MW01134366

BULLIES TO BUDDIES:

A Torah Guide for Turning
Your
Enemies into Friends

By Israel "Izzy" Kalman

BULLIES TO BUDDIES: A Torah Guide to Turning Your Enemies into Friends

Izzy Kalman, MS, NCSP

Copyright ©2019 by Israel (Izzy) Chaim Kalman
Revised edition, ©2020

All rights reserved. No part of this book may be reproduced, translated or transmitted in any form or by any means, electronic or mechanical, without the written permission of the Publisher. Exceptions are made for brief excerpts used in published reviews.

The Wisdom Pages
New York City
(718) 983-1333

Summary: Teaches youth how to use traditional Jewish wisdom to disarm bullying on their own and improve relationships in school and at home.

Based on author's earlier book, *Bullies to Buddies: how to turn your enemies into friends*

Audience: Grades 5-adult.
ISBN 0-9706482-4-3

Note to the reader: The advice in this volume is based on the author's four decades of experience as a school psychologist specializing in issues of bullying, aggression and anger control. The scenarios are fictional and any resemblance of characters to real persons is purely coincidental and unintentional.

The author offers consultation services, but your purchase or reading of this book does not create a consultant/client relationship. The information herein is not intended as a substitute for professional help. The author and publisher make no claims for its effectiveness and assume no responsibility or liability whatsoever on behalf of any purchaser or reader. If problems persist, the help of an appropriate and competent professional should be sought.

Cover illustration by Steve Ferchaud

Cover design and internal illustrations by Lola Edry

For more information, visit www.Bullies2Buddies.com.

TABLE OF CONTENTS

SECTION ONE: UNDERSTANDING LIFE

SECTION TWO: TREATING PEOPLE LIKE FRIENDS

SECTION THREE: SOME GOOD ADVICE

SECTION FOUR: SPECIFIC SITUATIONS

INTRODUCTORY NOTES FOR PARENTS AND EDUCATORS

I am excited to be publishing this version of my 2005 book, *Bullies to Buddies: How to Turn Your Enemies into Friends*, for the Torah-observant audience. My growing involvement with the *frum* population in the past few years has made it clear that I needed to produce a version of the book reflecting Torah values and concepts.

While I am not a Torah scholar, and have approached my psychological profession from a secular standpoint, I had an Orthodox Jewish education growing up and have always felt close to my people even during the years I was far from observance. Therefore, revising the book from the point of view of traditional Jewish thought was a welcome challenge. I hope it will be met with approval by our religious authorities. This was also a good opportunity to make needed improvements that will also be incorporated into an upcoming revision of the secular version of the book.

A few words about the concept of bullying are in order. First, what is bullying? It is perhaps the most confusing term to have entered the fields of education and psychology. The academic bullying experts have created a scientific-sounding definition of bullying involving intention to harm, repetitiveness and imbalances of power. However, the definition is highly problematic and, in practice, schools have a hard time determining if an act is bullying or not. To simplify the issue, the following is what I consider to be the most useful definition of bullying: *It's when you're getting picked on over and over again by the same people.* Everyone gets treated badly on occasion. Victims of bullying are the ones who are the regular targets of mean behavior. There are a couple of them in almost every classroom. These are the kids who are suffering terribly and need help.

Furthermore, as much as we worry about bullying in school, it actually occurs far more at home. In most families with one or more children, there is at least one child who gets picked on relentlessly by a sibling. It is tragic when siblings treat each other like enemies. Many children also feel bullied by their parents (and vice versa), to which they respond with ongoing disrespect and defiance towards the parents – a violation of the Fifth Commandment. This book teaches children how to stop being bullied both at school and at home by treating their perceived bullies with respect.

It is also important for teachers in school and parents at home to learn how they unwittingly promote aggression among children and how to reduce it with little effort. That is the purpose of my manual, *A Revolutionary Guide to Reducing Aggression Between Children,* available on IzzyKalman.com and Bullies2Buddies.com.

Now, a few words about the anti-bully movement. It is probably the most popular social cause in history, being eagerly embraced by most of the planet, including the world of

Jewish education. The idea of getting rid of bullies sounds so virtuous that hardly anyone in the world considers there might be anything wrong with it. To religious Jews, it also sounds like an extension of the Torah's efforts to get rid of evil. However, if the anti-bully movement were, indeed, morally sound, it would have solved the problem already. But the world has been engaging in an intensive campaign against bullying for two full decades and it's only become a bigger problem.

The truth is that this movement is a far cry from the teachings of our *chachamim*. A detailed explanation is beyond the scope of this introduction. But, in short, it violates the Torah's command of *ve'ahavta lere'acha kamocha* as well as Hillel's dictum: What is hateful to you, do not do to others. Unfortunately, the anti-bully movement fosters hatred, intolerance and emotional fragility, while instructing students to do to others what they hate having done to them, namely, to inform on others to the school staff.

Doing so immediately escalates hostilities between kids. If they are fortunate, the school will succeed in resolving the problem. If not, it will make it worse. And when the school involves the parents, as they are required to do today, the problem often escalates into a feud between families. In almost every yeshiva that has consulted with me, there are stories of painful and even vicious feuds between parents because of the alleged bullying among their children.

The anti-bully movement has also damaged the relationship between parents and the school. It has successfully indoctrinated parents with the belief that schools are responsible for guaranteeing that all children can attend without being bullied. This guarantee is impossible to fulfill. Research and plain experience show that the interventions schools are required to implement against bullying are at best minimally effective and can even lead to an increase. So how can schools guarantee a bully-free environment?

Unfortunately, parents, who usually have difficulty getting their own handful of children to always be nice to each other at home, now routinely blame the school for failing to make hundreds of children always be nice to each other. The harder the school tries to make the parents happy, the worse the bullying is likely to become. A feud between parents and the school then ensues. Parents are pulling their children out of yeshivas in growing numbers because of the unrealistic demand that they stop their children from being bullied.

If schools cannot be relied upon to prevent all bullying, is there an alternative? The best solution to bullying is obviously to teach children how to handle it on their own. Then they don't become snitches. They don't waste precious staff time with endless bullying complaints. Feuds between parents and between parents and schools are prevented. Teachers have more time for teaching. Students grow in self-esteem, resilience, popularity and happiness. And those students whose academic performance has fallen because of bullying go back to being good students. The only children we should actively protect are those who are truly incapable of learning to solve their social problems on their own because of limitations due to age or to neurologic and psychiatric conditions.

It would require too many pages to acknowledge all those who have contributed to the creation of this book. But special appreciation goes to Rabbi Yochonon Mayers, Professional Counselor, and Rabbi Yehoshua Levin-Landau, Mental Health Counselor, for first suggesting that I rework my book for Jewish readers and for a great deal of editing and guidance on religious matters. I also thank Rishe Deitsch, the distinguished editor of N'shei Chabad Newsletter, for encouraging my involvement with the Jewish world, for answering countless questions, and for proofreading this book with her eagle-sharp eyes.

I thank my daughter, Lola, for the great deal of time and effort she devoted to the 40 new illustrations within the book. I thank Steve Ferchaud, the magnificent artist who drew the cover illustration. I thank my children, most notably Yannai, for help with the final editing.

I thank Rabbi Nachman and Mrs. Chaya Segal for conveniently opening a Chabad Center a block away from my home in Staten Island, drawing me into a degree of involvement in shul life I hadn't had since my youth, and reconnecting me with my Lubavitch roots, as my elementary Jewish education was at the Lubavitcher Yeshiva of the Bronx. Thanks to the Segals, the series of events leading to this Jewish version of my book were unwittingly set in motion.

I thank my parents, Michael and Bracha Kalman, *aleihem hasholom,* Holocaust survivors who had the good sense to ensure I receive a Jewish education. I hope this book will give their *neshomos* an *Aliyah.*

And I thank my wife, Miriam, for being my devoted partner in the journey of life.

SECTION ONE:

UNDERSTANDING LIFE

If at any point you feel you need immediate help with your particular situation, jump to SECTION FOUR, Specific Situations, to look for advice on how to handle it. Then return to reading the book from the beginning.

THE MISERY OF BEING BULLIED

Do some kids treat you badly? Do they call you *meshugeneh, idiot or fatso?* Do they make fun of your mother or your *derech* or your level of *frumkeit or tsnius?* Do they spread mean rumors about you? Do they push you and hit you? Do they threaten to beat you up if you don't do what they want? Do they leave you out of groups or their lunch table? Do they write mean text messages to you, or post insulting things about you in social media? Are the popular students too embarrassed to even speak to you?

Have you tried everything to stop them? Calling them names back? Hitting them? Have you tried ignoring them, only to find the situation gets worse? Have you told on them to the *rebbe, morah* or *menahel?* And are you the one who usually gets in trouble even though they started with you?

Has yeshiva become a nightmare? Do you hate going because you know you'll be abused some more? Do you sit in class nervously wondering when the next insult will be hurled at you? Are you afraid to answer questions out loud because you may get laughed at? Instead of paying attention to your learning, do you spend time thinking up clever ways to respond to your bullies? And do you find that no matter how you respond, you end up looking and feeling bad?

Are you afraid to play outside or even go for a walk because of mean children?

Do you feel like a pressure cooker, so filled with anger that you are ready to explode? Do you dream about ways to get revenge against your bullies? Even worse, do you ever think it would be better not be alive at all, *chas veshalom,* just to escape the misery?

You may feel totally alone. It may seem like you are the only one who suffers from this terrible problem. But you're not. Being teased and bullied is one of the most common problems in the world. In almost every classroom in the world, one or two kids get teased and bullied every day.

Yes, there are thousands and thousands of kids who suffer just like you. And they all hate it.

But don't despair. No matter how short or tall or round you are, which branch of Yiddishkeit you follow, what part of the world your ancestors came from, what *minhagim* you follow, whether you have glasses or a big nose or ears, no one will continue picking on you after you learn the secrets revealed in this book.

Follow these simple instructions properly and you will begin defeating your bullies right away. Within a week, hardly anyone will bother you, and if they try, they'll feel like losers and quickly stop. Since you won't be getting anyone in trouble, you won't have to worry that they'll want revenge. When you are no longer bullied, the fear of going to yeshiva or hanging out in the neighborhood will be over for good. You will be able to go almost anywhere without being afraid.

Other good things will start happening. Life will be brighter, and you will feel calmer, happier and more confident than you have in a long time. Your sense of humor will improve and being around other people will be more fun. Your brothers and sisters will fight with you less and like you more. And your parents will be impressed with your growth in maturity.

THE BEST PERSON TO HELP YOU

Reuven came to my counseling office asking for help. He complained that students were making fun of him, pushing him around and playing practical jokes on him every day, and he couldn't stand it anymore. I discussed his situation with the *menahel,* who decided we should call an assembly, since this was a common problem in the yeshiva.

With 300 students facing me in the auditorium, I described how terrible it is to be cruel to other children. I explained that teasing hurts their feelings and bullying makes them terrified to come to school. I told them that *Hashem* says we should never tease or bully anyone and that we should not tolerate anyone who does. Whenever we see anyone picking on another student, we should immediately step in to stop the bully or get an adult to help.

One month later, Reuven returned to my office to thank me. He said everyone had become nice to him. The *menahel* called to tell me the assembly was a huge success and had convinced all the *talmidim* it was wrong to tease and bully. There was peace among the students. *Rebbeim* were able to spend all their time teaching instead of trying to stop children from fighting.

Are you thinking this story sounds too good to be true? Well, you are right! For thousands of years adults have been teaching children to be nice to each other and punishing them for being cruel. And for thousands of years children have continued to be cruel anyway. When adults try to stop children from bullying, sometimes they succeed. But often they find themselves running a court trial, with both children passionately arguing they were the victim and the other one the bully. The one who gets blamed and punished can't wait for the next opportunity to get even.

I'm sorry to bring you the bad news: If you are waiting for authorities around you to make people stop bullying you, you may find yourself suffering for the rest of your life. Bullying doesn't happen only among students. It happens among drivers on the road. It happens among adults at work. It happens within government. And it goes on in many families. Children and parents bully each other. Brothers and sisters bully each other. Many husbands and wives bully each other, too. So if you're looking forward to a bully-free life when you finish yeshiva, you are setting yourself up for disappointment.

No, I can't make the bullies of the world leave you alone, and neither can your parents, *rebbeim*, *mechanchim*, *menahalim*, friends or even the *beis din*.

The good news: Someone *does* have the power to make people stop tormenting you. That person is *you*.

Does this thought scare you? Don't worry. It probably won't be as hard as you think. I will show you how easy it is to make people stop picking on you and get them to like and respect you more. Best of all, you will be able to stop bullies without anyone else's help and without getting anyone in trouble. All by yourself, you will be able to turn your bullies into buddies. The rules you learn here will help you for the rest of your life.

A LITTLE STORY

Shimon goes for a walk and comes across an old house. In front stands a boy surrounded by dozens of pigeons. The boy is throwing pieces of bread on the sidewalk.

"What are you doing?" Shimon asks the boy.

"I'm making the pigeons go away," the boy answers.

"What do you mean, you're making them go away?" Shimon asks.

"Every morning, these birds come to our house. They're a terrible nuisance. The noise is terribly annoying, and the mess they leave all over the sidewalk is disgusting."

"So why are you throwing them bread?" Shimon asks.

"The only way to get rid of them is to throw them bread. As soon as the last crumb is finished, they suddenly can't stand being here. They all fly away and we don't see them again for a whole day!"

What does this story have to do with being teased and bullied? Lots! Keep reading and you'll soon understand.

WHY YOU ARE PICKED ON

Why do some people become the regular victims of bullies? There is only one reason, and it's always the same. The most important step in making bullying stop is to understand what makes it happen in the first place.

Miriam suffers because children call her four-eyes. She believes they taunt her because she wears glasses. But Miriam is wrong. Sure, she wears glasses, but that's not why she is taunted.

Yehudah is upset because he gets pushed every day in the hallway in yeshiva. He thinks the boys do it because they hate him. But Yehudah is wrong. Maybe some boys hate him, but that's not why they push him.

Levi is deeply offended when his classmates call him a *sheigetz*. It makes no sense to him because he is very *frum*. He thinks that maybe they do it because he eats *gebruchts* on Pesach. But Levi is wrong. Maybe they don't think it should be *mutar* to eat *gebruchts*, but that's not why they call him a *sheigetz*.

Peninah is miserable because girls spread rumors that she is stupid and gets bad grades. She does great in school and aces all her tests. Peninah believes the children are spreading rumors because they are jealous of her. But she's wrong. Maybe the other students wish they had her good grades, but that's not why they are talking about her.

Yitzy often cries because boys in yeshiva call him retarded. He thinks they are cruel to him because he is dyslexic and in a Special Ed class. But Yitzy is wrong. He has trouble learning how to read, but that is not why the boys call him retarded.

There is only one reason these people are being picked on, but none of them can see it. It's also the reason you are picked on, but you can't see it either.

This is what you do see. First, they bully you. Then you get mad and try to make them stop. It seems like they start the bullying and you are trying to make it stop. But the truth is the other way around. The real reason they bully you is *because* you become upset and try to stop them. Without realizing it, you are actually encouraging them to bully you.

"What do you mean, I am encouraging them to bully me!" you may be thinking, *"That doesn't make any sense! I'm not encouraging them to bully me. I'm only trying to make them stop!"*

But, believe it or not, you are encouraging them to bully you. You just can't see it because the bullying happens first and your efforts to stop the bullying come afterwards. We are used to thinking that the first event in time causes the second event. And here I

am, telling you that the second event - your attempt to stop the bullying - actually causes the bullying to happen. This sounds *meshuggeh* because the bullying happened first!

But it's not *meshuggeh.* When you get mad at children who call you names or push you, how do they feel? Are they sad about what they did? They sure aren't. If they felt bad about bothering you, they wouldn't do it. When they bother you and you get mad, they love it! They feel great! They can't get enough of it. You feel lousy, and the angrier you get, the more fun they have and the better they feel.

Whatever you do to stop the bullying only makes your bullies feel more powerful. They're thinking inside, *"Go ahead, try to stop me. You can't do it no matter how hard you try!"* Even if you try to hide your feelings, it's probably not working. Feelings are hard to hide for long. Chances are, your bullies know you are upset from the look on your face and the way you behave, and this makes them feel good.

You see, they are not calling you "fatso" because you are fat, or "four-eyes" because you wear glasses. They really don't care about how you look. All they really care about is having fun. We all like to have fun, and one great way to have fun is to drive someone else crazy.

Your tormentors have discovered they can tease you and make you upset. They look for your weak spots, the things you are really embarrassed about and don't want anyone to notice.

The things you are most sensitive about usually have some truth to them. For instance, you are short and the children discover you can't stand it when they call you "midget." Or you wear glasses, and it bugs you to be called "four-eyes." Or your mother is overweight, and you become enraged when they make "fat" jokes about her.

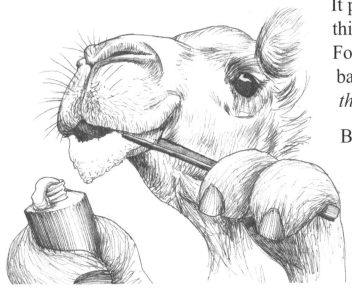

It probably wouldn't bother you if they said things that have nothing to do with the truth. For instance, if they said, "Your camel has bad breath," you'd just think, *"What a dumb thing to say. I don't even have a camel."*

But it really doesn't matter if what they say is true. All that matters is that it bothers you. If you are beautiful but get mad when they call you "ugly," they will keep calling you "ugly." If you are thin and you get upset when they call you "fatso," they will keep calling you "fatso." Whatever succeeds in annoying you is exactly what they are going to do again and again.

If words don't bother you but children discover you can't stand it when they put their hands on you, then pushing or hitting becomes a great way to defeat you. When you get mad, they have fun and want to do it again. And if you get in trouble because the *rebbe* catches you hitting them back, they have even more fun!

The only thing that matters to them is being able to upset you. This gives them pleasure, so it goes on and on, day after day after day, like a train going endlessly around a track. People pick on you, you get upset, and they have fun. They pick on you, you get upset, and they have fun.

The anger you feel when you are bullied is like the bread fed to those pigeons. You are attracting your bullies with crumbs of anger, thinking your anger is going to make them leave you alone. But your anger is exactly what keeps them coming back day after day. They look forward to it! You make them so happy when you get angry that they *never* want to stop bullying you.

Yes, believe it or not, you have been rewarding your bullies for making fun of you. They have so much fun when they torment you that they want to do it as much as possible.

TAKING RESPONSIBILITY

It may sound like I'm blaming you for being bullied. I'm not. You had no way of knowing what was really going on. The smartest children make the same mistake. So do adults. The same thing can go on in any relationship. Whether it is parents and children, husbands and wives, or brothers and sisters always arguing and fighting with each other, they are all making the same mistake. They don't realize that by getting upset they are practically *forcing* the other person to treat them in a way they can't stand. So, don't blame yourself. It's not your fault.

Don't blame anyone else, either. The only way you can improve your life is by taking responsibility and deciding to do something that will solve your problem. Once you can say to yourself, *"I finally understand how I've been contributing to my suffering,"* you can begin taking control of your life and start feeling much, much better.

Remember, you are not blaming yourself. You are taking responsibility. Blaming won't get you anywhere, but taking responsibility will.

THE YETZER HARA WITHIN

"Okay," you may be thinking, "maybe people pick on me because I get upset. But why would they enjoy upsetting me in the first place? It doesn't make sense! They are supposed to be *gitte Yidden*. What's wrong with them? Why do they act like animals?"

Well, if you think they are acting like animals, you happen to be right. They *are* acting like animals. Do you know why? It's because they *are* animals. And so are you. We all are.

This may sound *meshuggeh*, but I will do my best to explain it. I want to give you an introductory course on human psychology based on what I learned from our *chachamim*. Then it will be easier for you to understand what I teach you about bullying and how to get everyone to treat you better.

Our wise sages taught us that *Hashem* created human beings with two basic but very different parts.

One part is a temporary animal body that is controlled by a *nefesh habehamis*. Any biologist or doctor will tell you human bodies are built on the same model and from the same materials as animals. We have bones and blood and brains just like they do. We need to eat and sleep and breathe just like they do. That's why scientists perform experiments on animals to find cures for people. Our bodies are animal bodies.

If we don't give our animal body what it needs, we get sick and can die. *Hashem* wants us to live and be healthy, so he programmed the *nefesh habehamis* to feel pleasure when we do things that are good for the body and to feel pain when we do things that are bad for it. That's why eating, drinking and sleeping feel good, and putting our hands into fire hurts.

Hashem also wants to make sure that animals, including *b'nei adam*, do the basic behaviors that are necessary for them to stay alive, grow and have children of their own. So He programmed the *nefesh habehamis* to do them without having to be taught. Scientists have labeled these behaviors "instincts." That's why babies begin searching for mother's milk as soon as they are born. If someone had to teach them to do it, they would starve before they learned how.

Mothers also have instincts. Even animal mothers will risk their lives to make sure their children are safe. They take care of them without anyone having to instruct them to. Babies and mothers even have instincts that work together. Babies have the instinct to cry when they are uncomfortable, so that the mother will hear them. The mother's instinct is to want to stop the crying by making them comfortable. No one has to teach animals to do these things. They are instincts that *Hashem* programmed into the *nefesh habehamis*.

Among animals, there is no morality. This means that they don't make choices between doing good or evil. They just follow their instincts for survival. The reward for following the *nefesh habehamis* is feeling pleasure in this world.

But we humans aren't *only* animals. There is another part of us that is an eternal soul, a *nefesh Elokis*, or *neshamah*. It makes us different from all the other animals. Its goal is to get us to do *Hashem*'s will on Earth, to make the world a place fit for *Hashem*'s holiness. It is concerned with getting us to be moral, which means doing what is right in the eyes of *Hashem*. This requires us to study Torah, His instruction manual for life.

The *neshamah* exists forever and gets rewarded in *olam haba*, after we lead a moral life during the limited time that our body exists.

Morality requires the ability to choose between right and wrong, what we call *bechirah chofshis*.

While our bodies are animal bodies, they are different from the bodies of all other animals. There are several really important differences, but probably the most important one is that our brains are much bigger, especially the part of the brain called the cerebral cortex. This is the part of the brain that controls thinking and talking. No other animal thinks and communicates as well as *b'nei adam.*

Why did *Hashem* give us such a large brain? It's because it is necessary to house the *neshamah*. The *neshamah* is a spiritual entity but can only work in this world through a physical body. It needs a body with a big, powerful brain that can do the heavy-duty thinking and talking that is necessary to study Torah, to figure out what's right and wrong, and to teach it to others. Apes, the animals whose bodies are most similar to ours, have big brains, but not nearly as big as ours. Even though they are amazing examples of *Hashem*'s handiwork, can you imagine them trying to study a page of *gemora?* No, a *neshamah* cannot work in a chimpanzee brain. Only humans can truly understand what's right and wrong.

And that's where the *yetzer hara* comes into existence. Our *nefesh habehamis* is still programmed with instincts for physical survival. Sometimes the goals of the *nefesh habehamis* and the *neshamah* are the same. For example, if a baby is crying, the *neshamah* also wants the mother to go take care of it. The *nefesh habehamis* and the *neshamah* are both rewarded when the mother does this.

But often their goals are different. Let's say you're visiting friends and their mother is serving ice cream, but you just ate chicken a couple of hours ago. Your *nefesh habehamis* tells you to ask for a big portion but your *neshamah* tells you that you will be doing an *aveirah* if you eat it. Now you have to make a choice. You may hear a voice in your head coming up with reasons why it really is okay to eat the ice cream. Maybe it tells you that nothing terrible is going to happen to you if you eat it just this one time, or that chicken isn't really meat. This is the *yetzer hara* at work, trying to convince you to do what *halachah* says is wrong. The *yetzer hatov,* on the other hand, tells you it's better to pass on the ice cream. It can be very hard to fight off the *yetzer hara*, especially if the ice cream is our favorite flavor or brand.

The *yetzer hara* is also at work in our social lives. Let's say you are planning a birthday party, but there are a couple of children in your class who you think are *nebbishes* and will make your party "uncool." You realize they'll probably feel terrible if they're the only ones not invited. A voice in your head starts trying to convince you why it's better not to invite them. That is the *yetzer hara* at work.

We all have a *yetzer hara* that we constantly need to be aware of. Very few people are absolute *tzadikim*. We all give in to the *yetzer hara* at times, and often we aren't even aware that we're doing it. If other children are being mean to you, please realize that it is their *yetzer hara* at work, and we all have one. They are not necessarily any worse than you and me. In fact, you will be learning in this book that if other children are constantly picking you on, it's probably because your own *yetzer hara* is also at work and you aren't even aware of it.

You will also learn how to use your *yetzer hatov* to get people to stop bullying you. You may even bring out their *yetzer hatov* and help them become better people.

THE VERBAL BULLYING EXPERIMENT

I want to tell you about a game I have played with thousands of people of all ages and backgrounds. It is like a scientific experiment, and it has taught me so much about human nature. You should play this game (experiment) with a few "subjects." (A "subject" in science means someone on whom you conduct an experiment.) You can use friends or relatives as your subjects. The experiment will do two things for you. 1) It will give you terrific practice in making bullying stop, so that you can get started even before you finish reading the whole book. 2) It will help you understand secrets of human nature. (You may even want to turn this into a science experiment for school!)

Step 1: Tell your subject:

"I am going to play a game with you. Your job is to insult me and my job is to make you stop. But don't stop or you lose. Don't worry about really hurting my feelings. It's just a game and I want you to play to win."

(You must *truly* be ready to hear their insults without getting upset.)

When the subject insults you, act angry and demand that they stop. Say things like:
- Shut up!
- That's not true!
- You can't talk to me like that!
- Show me respect!

- If you don't shut your mouth, you're really going to be sorry!

Do you think your subjects will stop? No way! Most of them will smile and laugh and insult you even more. The angrier you become, the more they will enjoy insulting you. After a while, when it has become obvious that the subject isn't stopping, say, "I give up. You win."

Step 2: Say to your subject:

"We're going to play the game again. Your job is to insult me and my job is to make you stop."

This time, instead of getting angry and trying to stop them, stay calm and make it clear that it is okay with you if they insult you all day long. You can say things like:

- Thanks for your opinion.
- If you like to insult me, please be my guest.
- What else is wrong with me?
- That is a good insult.
- Do you believe it? (If they say, "Yes," answer, "You can believe it if you wish.")

You should discover that almost everyone responds the same way. They have fun when you get angry and feel frustrated when you don't.

Our *nefesh habehamis* makes it fun for us to enjoy driving people crazy. You may think you are different, but if I had the chance to play the game with you and had you insult me, I guarantee that you, too, would enjoy it when I get mad and feel foolish when I don't. It's not only your "bullies" who enjoy it. We all do. As I often say, "The bullies 'r' us!"

Note: Just in case you think I am implying that we are all *resha'im* – evil people who enjoy hurting others – let me reassure you I'm not. If your subjects in the game believed they were truly hurting you, their *yetzer hatov* would make them stop. But they know it's only a game and that you're not really getting hurt. Still, it's only fun for them the first time, when you are getting upset. The second trial was also a game, but it's no fun for them when you are calm and nice. What the game does is allow the *yetzer hara* to show itself by "temporarily disabling" the *yetzer hatov.* And the *yetzer hara* enjoys getting you upset, so the subjects smile and laugh.

THE PHYSICAL BULLYING EXPERIMENT

Here is another experiment you should do with a few subjects. It explores physical aggression. Be careful not to change the order of the two steps.

Step 1: Ask the subject to stand next to you. Then say, "Give me a push." After they push you, act like nothing happened and go back to where you were standing. They will probably just stand there, looking a bit confused. They may give you another little push, but probably do nothing after that.

Step 2: After waiting several seconds, say again, "We're going to do it over. Give me a push." This time when they push you, push back and yell, "Stop pushing me!" They will probably smile or laugh, and might even push you again.

This experiment shows that if you do nothing when people provoke you, most of them feel foolish and stop. You win by ending the assault, even though you did absolutely nothing. The second time, even though you "stand up for yourself," the other person wins and has fun, and a fight may be set in motion.

THE GAME OF LIFE

If you are like most young people, you enjoy playing games. Playing is fun. You know exactly what you are doing and why. And you know when you are winning and when you are losing because the rules are clear.

You may not be used to thinking of life as a game, but it is. Just like in games, there are rules for winning and losing in life. If you know the rules well, you have a better chance of winning. If you win in the game of life you feel good, and if you lose, you feel bad.

If the same people are bullying you repeatedly, you have probably noticed that they enjoy picking on you, and it makes you miserable. That's because they are winning and you are losing. You've been trying very hard to win, but whatever you've been doing hasn't been working.

BULLYING The Board Game!!!
Fun for the Whole Family!!
No Batteries Required...
A Great Shabbos Activity!!!

The bullying doesn't seem like a game to you. That's because your bullies never got together with you and said, "Let's play this game. We're going to bully you and if you can stop us, you win." But that doesn't mean they're not playing a game with you. They are trying to defeat you and they are succeeding.

It is very hard to win a game if you don't know the rules. We end up following our instincts. Unfortunately, our instincts can make us lose.

The purpose of instincts is to help us succeed, to win in life. So why would your instincts make you lose against your bullies? The reason is that your instincts belong to the *nefesh habehamis,* which guides animal behavior.

Animals live in the lawless world of nature, where life is very dangerous. In nature there are no governments, police and courts. Let's say you and I are animals, and you are trying to eat me for dinner. Can I tell you, "Hey, get your hands off me! It's against the Torah! I'm going to call the police on you and then get my lawyer to sue you!"? Of course not! You'll think, "What is Torah? What are police? What's a lawyer?" You'll be happily eating me and no one will be coming along to arrest you.

Animals, therefore, need to be able to do their own fighting and protection. If we live in nature, I need to be willing to tear you to pieces before you tear me to pieces. Otherwise I will be a big loser. And that is the kind of life for which our *nefesh habehamis* is programmed to try to win.

But humans are different from other animals. We have a *neshamah* and live in civilization, not in the lawless world of nature. You learned in *Parshas Noach* that there was a time several thousand years ago, when everyone went back to living according to their animal instincts. This made us evil in the eyes of *Hashem,* so he brought the *mabul* to wipe us out and have us start over again. *Hashem* gave mankind *sheva mitzvos b'nei Noach* so that we would stop acting like animals. One of those seven *mitzvos* is to set up courts of law. Instead of following our *nefesh habehamis* and fighting each other physically when we have disagreements, we go to a *beit din*, where wise judges decide who is right and who is wrong and how to resolve our disputes. You can no longer just steal from me or eat me for dinner and expect to get away with it.

Later, *Hashem* gave Jews the Torah so we could become holier, like Him, and help make the whole world more holy and civilized as well.

Today, we win by following the laws that *Hashem* gave. However, our *nefesh habehamis* didn't disappear. We still have it, and instead of helping us win the game of life, it often makes us lose. That's because it's following the rules for winning in nature, and those rules are very different from the rules for winning in civilization.

I will be teaching you in this book how our *nefesh habehamis* makes it easy for our bullies to make us fall into traps and defeat us. I will also be teaching you how to use the principles of the Torah, as explained by our *chachamim*, in order to win the game of life and defeat your bullies.

In nature, the *nefesh habehamis* usually leads to one side winning and the other side losing. The nice thing about the *neshamah* is that when we follow it by living according to Torah, both sides usually win, too. Everybody becomes happier and the world becomes a better place!

You will also discover that knowing the rules for winning in civilization will give you a big advantage over your bullies. That's because they don't really understand the rules for winning in civilization, either. They just follow the instincts of their *nefesh habehamis*. When you know the rules for winning and they don't, it becomes almost impossible to defeat you!

What is the most important component to becoming a winner in the game of life? Power. What kind of power? People power. Having people on your side will give you power. Having people against you will weaken you.

IS POWER BAD?

You may think power is bad. After all, your bullies have power over you, and that sure doesn't feel good. Maybe you've heard adults say that people who want power are evil. That's because they think power means hurting others or taking unfair advantage of them.

If you believe power is bad you are handicapping yourself. You will have no chance against someone who likes power and knows how to get it.

Remember that the *nefesh habehamis* has instincts that help our animal body stay alive and healthy, and that following our instincts is accompanied by pleasure. One of the instincts is for power. If we don't have enough power, others can defeat or destroy us. That's why being powerful feels good, and being powerless feels bad. If having power didn't feel good, we wouldn't try to have it, and we would be easily defeated.

Perhaps you think of power as beating people up, and you don't want to be a violent person. However, there are many things you do for power *without* injuring anyone. Just think about it. Do you ever argue with your parents, say, over what time to go to bed or when to come home from spending time with friends? Do you ever try to force a brother or sister out of your room? You may not have realized it, but it's power that you want. Whenever you find yourself in an argument or a fight, you are trying to overpower the other person.

Even when you are doing things everyone considers good, you are actually seeking power. Do you want good grades in school? Good grades are power. Get higher grades than your classmates, and your teachers and parents will like you, admire you, and try to help you achieve your goals in life. Good grades will get you into better yeshivas and seminaries, and help you get the best jobs so you can earn lots of money. Do you want lots of money? Well, money is power. With money you pay other people to help you and to make things for you. If you would rather be rich than poor, that means you want power. Don't feel guilty about it. That's just the way life is. Even yeshivas need money so they can pay their bills and stay open.

Perhaps to your surprise, you will soon see the best way to have power is not by being mean to people but by being nice. So don't worry about power being bad. It's *not* having power that is bad.

WHY YOU NEED POWER

Okay, so maybe power isn't bad. But why do we need to control others?

The reason is simple. Can you grow, pick and prepare all the food you need for yourself? Can you make your own clothing? Can you make your own house and furniture and toys? Can you teach yourself Torah and everything you need to know? Of course not! No one can. The only way we can survive is by having others help us.

This is especially true if you are a child, because you aren't able to perform many of the tasks critical to your survival. You probably don't realize it, but there are *avodim* working for you round-the-clock without even being told to. These slaves are your parents, and possibly your grandparents or other adult relatives. They feed you, clothe you, give you a roof over your head, provide you with entertainment, drive you around, take care of you when you are sick or hurt, and clean up after you. They do much more for you than you do for them. They don't get paid for their work, and they never stop being responsible for you. And there's a good chance that instead of appreciating everything they do for you, you just get mad at them when they don't give you what you want. You may feel like they try to boss you around. But if you think about it, you will realize you have much more control over them than they have over you.

Even adults need to have power over others because they can't make everything they need to survive. They go to work and do things for others. Then they get paid so they can pay others to do things for them. In order for society to exist, people have to give power to others and get power over others. Power over others is necessary for you and for me.

THE CARROT OR THE STICK

There are two ways to get power. They are known as "the carrot" and "the stick." Almost all acts of getting power fall into one of these two categories, which refer to ways for getting a stubborn mule to pull your cart. You can dangle a carrot in front of the animal and it will move forward, trying to reach the food. Or you can hit its backside with a stick and it will move forward to avoid being hit again.

It's the same thing with people. You can get power over them by making them feel good (offering them the carrot) or by hurting them (hitting them with the stick). If you make them feel good, they will want to do things for you to make you happy. If you hurt them,

18

they will fear you and do things for you so that you won't hurt them again.

The carrot approach has advantages over the stick. If you do things that make people feel good, they will like you and try to make you happy in return. They won't feel you are controlling them because they are acting from their own choice. It is also safe because you won't be causing anyone to seek revenge.

If you hurt people, they may give you power over them because they are afraid of you. But they will hate you for hurting them and resent you for controlling them. It also puts you in danger because they will be on the lookout for any opportunity to get even.

In case you haven't realized it yet, the "carrot" is the buddy way to have power and the "stick" is the bully way. Making people feel good turns them into your friends and making them feel bad turns them into your enemies.

You may think you are a good person and that you don't use the bully way to achieve power, but chances are you use it much more often than you think. Do you ever yell or whine or pout when your parents aren't giving you what you want? Do you ever hit your brothers and sisters, or call them names? Do you ever tell your friends you are not going to get together with them if they don't do the activity you want? Do you ever tell the *morah* when kids bother you in school? All these are examples of using the stick.

Unfortunately, in real life we can't always use only the carrot. This is especially true when people have to make others obey them. This includes *mechanchim* and parents and bosses. Shlomo HaMelech said, *"Chosech shivto sonay b'no."* If you have no fear of your parents, it will be very hard for them to stop you from doing bad things. Your *mechanchim* have to make you work hard many hours a day in school and then at home. They couldn't get you to do all this work just by being nice to you (the carrot). They also have to make you afraid of lousy grades and punishments (the stick).

No one uses only the buddy way or the bully way. We use both. Most of us, though, don't even think about which one we are using. We just go along with our feelings at the moment, or act by habit without considering if it's smart. Far too often, we use the bully way. That's what gets us in trouble. People treat us badly because we don't even realize we are using the stick.

To become a winner, you have to start thinking about when to use the carrot and when to use the stick. First, you will need to recognize the ways you have been using the stick without being aware of it. Then you will have to replace the stick with the carrot. The better you get at giving carrots, the less you will need sticks. You will find people like you better, are nicer to you, and do more for you. (And they won't even realize that you are influencing them!)

THE POWER RULES IN NATURE

If using the carrot is so much better than the stick, why do so many of us use the stick? Why do we often get angry and become mean instead of always behaving nicely to each other? Why are there bullies that make us miserable?

It's because we have an animal body with a *nefesh habehamis*. *Hashem* programmed it to help animals survive in the lawless world of nature. The *nefesh habehamis* doesn't understand that today we live by *sheva mitzvos b'nei Noach* and the Torah, and behaves as though we are animals in nature. Let's look at what that life must be like.

In nature, "might makes right." There are no policemen and judges, so we would have to do our own fighting and protection. If you are stronger than your opponent, you win. Therefore "the stick" is very important.

Animal groups have a leader that the rest follow, and the member who is strongest usually gets to be the leader. Most members would love to be the leader because there are benefits. If you are the leader, everyone else in the group is afraid of you and shows you respect. You could boss them around because they don't want you to beat them up. You get your choice of food and sleeping places. You get to decide who is going to be your partner in having children (there are no *shadchanim* in nature).

By the way, there is a good chance you have experienced the desire of the *nefesh habehamis* to be physically strongest, especially if you are a boy. Even *frum* boys wish they could be like Shimshon HaGibor, and have contests to find out who is strongest among them.

If you are a female in nature you have to be tough, too. You need to defend yourself and your children from other dangerous animals and maybe to hunt them, as well.

If we are threatened or attacked by other animals, including members of our own group, our *nefesh habehamis* reacts with anger in the attempt to scare them off. If we succeed in making them afraid, they leave us alone, and we are safe until the next time we're threatened. If the enemies are not scared off, and we can't escape, we need to have the drive to fight them and destroy them before they destroy us.

But don't think the stick is the only way to achieve power in nature. If you are the leader and all you do is beat people up and act selfishly, the rest of us would hate you. If there is a tough guy we liked better, we would support his efforts to knock you off and become the leader instead of you.

If you lack physical strength and can't get power by using the stick, you could still have a high position in the group by getting power with the carrot. If you figure out ways to make lots of group members like you, then their power becomes your power. It's what's called today, "being popular." When you are threatened, attacked, sick or injured, the rest of us would gladly step in to help you. So, even in nature, you would have to know how to use the carrot in order to have power. If you are generous, considerate, and appreciative to your followers, they will support you for a long time.

Have you noticed that even among Jewish children there is a strong desire to be popular? That comes from our *nefesh habehamis*. For girls to be leaders, it is not so important that they be physically strong. The way to have power is to be popular, to have other people on their side. The most popular girl is often called the "queen bee." Isn't it interesting that she's named after an animal? She is envied, admired and even feared by the rest

of the group. The queen bee has a lot of power because she is able to make other girls do what she wants, even to turn them against each other or to put *cherem* on one or more of the other girls in the group.

Since the carrot and the stick are essential for survival, *Hashem* programmed the *nefesh habehamis* with instincts to use them both. That's why we feel good when other people like us, and we also feel good when others are too afraid of us to try to hurt us.

THE POWER RULES IN CIVILIZATION

While our *nefesh habehamis* is programmed for life in nature, we live in civilization, where life is very different. To survive in nature, animals just take what they need because *Hashem* provides it for them right in their environment. But we humans are dependent upon each other for almost everything we have. We farm together to grow our food. We work together to build houses and make all the clothing, furniture and tools we need. Most of us live in crowded towns and cities and there are many more opportunities for getting into each other's way, for fighting and for arguing. We can't just go around living by "might makes right" or we'd be fighting each other physically all the time. There'd be lots of pain and bloodshed, and we wouldn't get much done. Many of us might not even survive.

In Civilization, therefore, we need to live by laws, which are rules for handling or preventing conflict without violence. It's important that the laws be fair so that we will all agree to live by them. When we have a conflict with someone, instead of having a physical battle to see who gets his way, we work it out by the rules. We have law enforcement systems, including police and courts, so we can catch and punish people who don't play by the rules.

In civilization, therefore, "justice makes right." That's why the Torah tells us, *Tzedek tzedek tirdof* (Devarim 16:20). *Hashem* wants us to be just, and that's why our *yetzer hatov* wants it as well. Justice makes life better for everyone. And it gets our *neshamah* rewarded in *olam haba*.

Living by laws makes humans the most successful of all animals. In nature, the number of members of a species is limited by the amount of food they can find. But because we are the smartest of all animals, we are able to figure out how nature works and use it to our advantage. We are not limited by the amount of food we can find because we learned how to grow food. Scientists estimate that around the time the Torah was given on *Har Sinai,* there were around 50 to 100 million people in the whole world. Now there are over 7 billion. That means that for every person who was alive then, there are around 100 today. That's only possible because of laws. In fact, we are so good at producing food that this is the first period in the history of the world that even poor people can be fat! The biggest problem for most people today is not "Where is my next meal going to come from?" but "How do I stop eating so much?"

Civilization makes it against the law to use violence to get our way. If we use the stick too hard, instead of getting more power, we get in trouble. We can be arrested and punished and become big losers. Civilization also means we can live without fear that our neighbors are going to hurt us. They know we can call the police on them and then they lose.

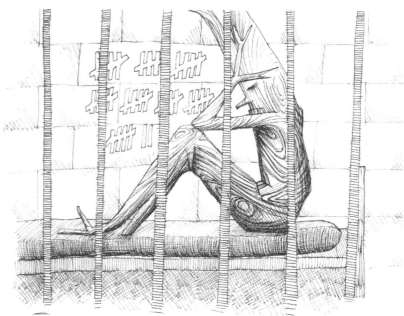

Civilization makes it possible for us to become leaders without risking injury. You don't become president of a country by becoming the best boxer. The carrot has become a lot more important for getting power. Today you become a leader not by making people afraid of you but by convincing them that you can make their lives better. In our personal lives, too, the better we are at making people happy, the more powerful we become.

WHY PEOPLE BULLY EACH OTHER

If civilization makes it possible to have power without harming others, why are people so mean to each other? Why is there so much bullying going on?

It's because civilization didn't make our *nefesh habehamis* disappear. When we're in a situation that requires us to choose between following the *nefesh habehamis* or the *neshamah*, the *yetzer hara* will try to convince us to follow the *nefesh habehamis* to get the immediate pleasure. It will push us to gain power by hurting and scaring people. If you aren't sure about this, just look at how quickly most of us get angry when people don't give us what we want. Do you think we're offering carrots when we're angry?

Anger is not nice. It doesn't make people feel good or turn them into friends. It is aggressive behavior. It's the attempt to scare them off or beat them up. In civilization, we continue getting angry even though it almost always makes the situation worse. It's because our *nefesh habehamis* is programmed for the dangerous life in nature, when getting angry was necessary for defeating real enemies.

The younger we are, the more the *nefesh habehamis* controls us. When we were toddlers, practically all of us would bully our parents by screaming, hitting or throwing objects at them to make them do what we want. We would also do these things to our brothers, sisters, cousins and friends. No one taught us these aggressive behaviors. We were just doing what came naturally. In fact, our parents worked hard to teach us not to do them. They were always busy trying to teach us to be nice, to follow our *yetzer hatov.*

As we grow up, we discover being mean gets us punished but being nice and obeying rules of fairness makes people like us and want to be nice to us. So the *yetzer hatov* gets strengthened and we learn to be less aggressive.

Some of us, though, prefer to continue using force to be powerful. Their *nefesh habehamis* enjoys the power of bossing others around and scaring them. If we were animals in nature, such individuals might become our leaders. In civilization, though, many of them get in trouble so often that they end up hating society. Some of them join gangs, take up criminal activities and serve time in jail.

The really smart ones, though, figure out how to be tough and scary without getting in trouble. They get good grades and act nicely and respectfully when adults are watching, so adults don't believe they are capable of being mean to other children. If their victim tells the teacher on them, their friends will testify that the victim is lying and then the victim may be the one who gets punished.

Because they are successful in school and know how to use power, they may go on to get important jobs when they are adults. They may end up with leadership positions in companies, labor unions or government. Some might become soldiers or policemen or firefighters, open a business or do other things that require toughness and daring. Though we may think all bullies are terrible, the truth is that even in civilization they are needed for positions that require fearlessness. We need to realize that they also have a *yetzer hatov*, which might have gotten stronger over the years. They may no longer be using their power for the pleasure of scaring people but because they want to protect and help them.

There's one big disadvantage caused by civilization. While civilization makes life safer for you, it also makes it easier for people to bully you and drive you crazy. In nature for people to defeat you, they have to be stronger and meaner than you. But in civilization, they can be weaker and still bully you. How? By using your *nefesh habehamis* against you.

This is how it works: The bullies pick on you. You feel under attack, so your *nefesh habehamis* immediately responds by getting angry, hoping to scare them away. In nature, they would be afraid of you if you were stronger than them. But in Civilization they are not really afraid of you because they know it is against the law for you to injure them, and they know that you know this, too! So you get angrier and angrier in the attempt to win, but don't realize that the angrier you get, the more foolish you look. And if you get so angry that you hit them, they get you in trouble and you become a really big loser. So even though you are physically stronger than they are, they can still defeat you by getting you angry and driving you crazy!

Section One Quiz

1. The best person in the world to make bullies leave you alone is:
  a. The President of the United States
  b. Your mother or father.
  c. The *rebbe*.
  d. The *menahel*.
  e. You.

2. Victims continue to get picked on by bullies because:
  a. They look different from other people.
  b. They are not as smart as those picking on them.
  c. They get upset by the bullying.
  d. The yeshiva does nothing to stop bullies.

3. When you get angry at bullies, the bullies are most likely to:
  a. Feel bad about what they did and apologize.
  b. Have fun and want to bother you again.
  c. Get scared of you and leave you alone.
  d. Cry.

4. Bullying happens:
  a. To children in school.
  b. To children at home.
  c. To adults.
  d. To people of all ages and relationships.

5. The first step to solving problems with other people is:
  a. Blaming them for making you feel bad.
  b. Blaming yourself.
  c. Figuring out what you are doing wrong.
  d. Complaining to adults.

6. When people call you names and you don't try to stop them:
  a. They will feel like losers.
  b. They will feel like winners.
  c. They will try to break your nose.
  d. They will tell the *menahel* on you.

7. If someone pushes you and you push back, the person will probably:
    a. Feel bad for having pushed you.
    b. Thank you.
    c. Shake your hand.
    d. Push you back even harder.

8. To win the game of life, it is most important to:
    a. Hurt people.
    b. Cheat.
    c. Treat people like friends.
    d. Make people scared of you.

9. Trying to get good grades is:
    a. Only for cowards and losers.
    b. A waste of time.
    c. A good way to make people hate you.
    d. A good way to have power.

10. Which one of the following words most accurately describes what your parents are for you:
    a. Slaves.
    b. Masters.
    c. Playmates.
    d. Shopkeepers.

11. Being able to beat people up is most important for survival in:
    a. Modern Civilization.
    b. School.
    c. Societies without laws.
    d. Camp.

12. In Modern Civilization:
    a. "Justice makes right."
    b. "Might makes wrong."
    c. "Justice makes wrong."
    d. "Might makes right."

13. If we were living before the *mabul*, children who were best at fighting and scaring people would probably grow up to be:

    a. Weaklings.

    b. Cooks.

    c. Healers.

    d. Leaders.

14. To defeat others in Modern Civilization:

    a. You have to be able to beat them up.

    b. You only need to be able to get them mad.

    c. You need to have nicer clothing than they do.

    d. You need to have bigger muscles than they do.

SECTION TWO:
TREATING PEOPLE LIKE
FRIENDS

THE TORAH "ON ONE FOOT"

It would be really great if we had a rule that let us know the right way to treat people without having to think too hard about each situation. Fortunately our Torah has given us such a rule.

Rabbi Akiva taught us that *ve'ahavta le-re'acha kamocha*, *Love your fellow as yourself*, is the all-encompassing principle of the Torah. That means that all of the Torah involves loving other people just as we love ourselves.

Hillel is famous for teaching us another way of understanding how the Torah wants us to treat each other. A non-Jew came to the great rabbi Shammai, wanting to become a Jew. He said, "Teach me the whole Torah while standing on one foot" (meaning very quickly). Shammai impatiently chased him away with a stick.

The same man then went to the rabbi Hillel and asked him to teach him the whole Torah on "one foot." Hillel said to him, "Don't do to others what you hate them doing to you. That is the whole Torah. All the rest is commentary."

It is obvious that if everyone lived by Akiva's and Hillel's principles, life would be wonderful. People wouldn't fight. Bullying wouldn't happen. But we have known the principles for thousands of years. So why doesn't everyone follow them by now?

It's because most of us don't really know what these principles come to teach us, which is why we often have trouble getting along.

Almost everyone thinks that these Torah teachings instruct us not be mean to anyone, and to always be nice. But isn't this obvious? Do we really need a Torah to tell us that we should be nice to people and not be mean?

So I will explain to you why we need these principles.

Of course it's important to be nice. Your parents and *mechanchim* are always teaching you to be nice. It is so easy to be nice to people when they are nice to us.

But people aren't always nice. Sometimes they are mean on purpose. But often they are mean and they don't even realize it. I bet that people have sometimes accused you of being mean to them and you were totally surprised. So what are we supposed to do when people aren't nice to us? What should we do when they bully us? That's the hard part – knowing what to do when people treat us badly.

Because we are always taught that it's good to be nice and bad to be mean, this is what happens when someone is mean to us. We think, *"How dare they treat me that way? They're supposed to be nice to me! I am always nice to everyone! How can they treat me so badly?"* So we get angry with them. We want revenge. We want to get them punished.

So what the Torah teaches us is to love them like we love ourselves. It means we should be considerate and respectful to them because we want them to be considerate and respectful to us. We shouldn't be angry and mean back because we hate it when they are angry and mean to us.

You might think that it's crazy to be nice to people when they are mean to you. Won't you be a big loser? Won't people think you are a *nebbish* or a *naar* who can be easily taken advantage of, so they'll keep on being mean?

The answer is, "Probably not." You will actually come out being a winner. You will be in control. They will respect and like you more. And they will also win. Everyone wins when you live by *ve'ahavta lere'acha kamocha*.

This is how it works. When someone is nice to you, do you feel like being mean back, or nice? Nice, of course. And when someone is mean to you, do you feel like being nice back, or mean? Mean.

Everyone is like that. When people are nice to us, we feel like being nice back. When they're mean to us, we feel like being mean back. Nobody taught this to us. It's our *nefesh habehamis* at work. It is programmed to treat others the way they treat us because that helps animals survive in the world of nature, in the jungle.

If we are animals in the jungle and you are nice to me, it means you are probably on my side. You are safe. I can be nice back to you and it will be good for both of us. It would be foolish for me to be mean to you because then I will turn you into an enemy and you might hurt me.

On the other hand, if you are mean to me in nature, you are probably looking to hurt me for some reason, maybe even to eat me for dinner. If I am not able to escape from you,

I had better be really mean back to you or you are going to eat me and you won't even say a *bracha!*

But we aren't animals in the jungle. We are human beings in civilization. I don't have to be afraid of you because you aren't looking to eat me for dinner. No matter how angry you might be with me, you aren't going to try to injure me physically because you know I can call the police and get you in big trouble.

If I listen to my *nefesh habehamis,* and I treat everyone the way they treat me, I will end up having a lot of enemies. Whenever people are mean to me, I will be mean back. Then they'll be mean again to me because I was just mean to them. We'll probably go back and forth being mean, and turn into enemies. We'll actually be pushing each other to become worse people.

So instead of listening to my *nefesh habehamis,* I will listen to my *nefesh haElokis,* my *neshamah,* which tells me to love you as I love myself. You know what will probably happen? Exactly what *Hashem* wants. It will create a win/win situation. It's because your *nefesh habehamis* is also programmed to treat *me* the way I treat *you.* Since I am now being nice to you, after a while you are probably going to be nice back to me. Now we're friends instead of enemies!

Instead of pushing you to become a worse person, I'm actually helping you become a better person.

This idea is so wonderful that almost all religions in the world have adopted it, and even people who don't believe in *Hashem* follow it. In recent times it has been named The Golden Rule.

The more that people understand and follow *ve'ahavta lere'acha kamocha,* the more good there will be in the world. Little by little, everyone will become better, and who knows? Maybe it will make the Moshiach come!

Throughout your life, if you are ever unsure about how to handle a problem with another person, ask: *"Am I loving this person as myself?"* or *"Would I like it if they were doing to me what I am doing to them?"* If the answer is "Yes," you will probably solve the problem. If the answer is "No," you will probably get bad results and should change your strategy.

It is not always obvious how to use *ve'ahavta lere'acha kamocha.* This book should make it clearer for you.

REALIZE THAT NO ONE IS PERFECT

Before you continue, it is important to realize that no one is perfect. That simple bit of understanding will make it easier for you to get along with people, including those who bully you.

If people are mean to you, you probably think badly of them. Remember that the *nefesh habehamis* is programmed to treat others the way they treat us. If you think badly of them, they are likely to think badly of you, too. Then they will treat you badly. But if you think well of them, they will probably think well of you, too.

But how can you think well of people when they are treating you badly? By asking yourself, "Am I perfect?" You will have to answer, "No." You can be a genius, the best-looking person in your class, and the best athlete. Still, you are not perfect. Even the greatest *tzadikim* will tell you they are not perfect, and they won't be lying. Everybody has flaws that can use fixing.

If you are getting mad at people, it's because deep down you believe they need to be perfect. They need to be absolute *tzadikim* who know how to treat everyone in the absolute best way. But that's impossible because almost no one is a perfect *tzadik*, and there will always be people who treat you in a way you don't like.

However, once you realize that you are not perfect, and that you sometimes treat people badly, you can no longer expect others to be perfect, either. You won't get so upset with them for treating you imperfectly because you'll realize you're not necessarily better than they are. And it will be a lot easier for you to follow the advice in the rest of this book.

STOP THINKING OF PEOPLE AS "BULLIES"

In Pirkei Avos 1:6, Yehoshua ben Pirchiya counsels us to "judge everyone favorably"– *hevey dan kol adam lekav z'chus.* This is wonderful advice.

Do you want to stop being a victim? Then starting right now, stop thinking of people as bullies. When we think of people as bullies, are we judging them favorably? Would *you* like to be thought of as a bully? Of course not! A bully is a *rasha,* an evil person who enjoys making others suffer. It is certainly appropriate to think of people like Haman and Hitler (*yemach shemam*) as *resha'im,* but if you think of other kids in school or in your neighborhood as *resha'im,* you are not following the advice of our Torah.

You may be thinking, *"But everyone is talking about bullies today. There are anti-bully organizations and laws, and even our Yeshiva is talking about bullies. Even this book is called Bullies to Buddies."*

The truth is that most of the Gentile (non-Jewish) world has been talking a lot about bullies for about two decades. Scholars in universities are doing research on bullies and telling us that a high percentage of people are bullies. More and more books are being published about bullies. Since highly educated and respected people are teaching us about bullies, everyone thinks it must be the right thing to do, so even yeshivas have started to think of people as bullies. But it wasn't always so. In all the years that I went to school in the 1950's through the 1970's, none of our teachers or principals ever used the words "bully" and "bullying" to describe us and our behavior. Maybe they thought of a mean kid in the neighborhood who would attack Jewish kids as a bully, but they never used it about us.

Some of the ideas developed by the Gentile world are in accordance with the Torah world, and they turn out to be good. But some of the ideas don't. After many years, we may realize that the idea was a mistake. One of those ideas is calling people "bullies." Could you imagine the Torah wanting us to look around us and think of any kid we're not getting along with as a *rasha?* Do you know of any *seforim* or great *rabbonim* that do that? No! They all teach us to think well of people, to judge them favorably.

So why do I use the word "bully" in this book? It's because everyone today wants to know what to do about bullies. If I don't use the word, who is going to want to read my book? They'll look for other books about bullies. So even though I use the word, I am actually hoping to convince people to stop using it.

Once in a while in this book, I use the term "your bullies." It's because I don't mean that "bullies" is what they really are. It only means that they are the people who you experience as being bullies. I hope that after you finish reading this book, you will hardly ever think of anyone as a bully again. And I hope even more strongly that you will find that all the people in your life are "your buddies." But as long as you think of people as bullies, you are going to hate them and treat them like enemies. So they will continue to be your enemies — and continue to make you miserable.

It may seem obvious that your bullies are bad and you are good. But do you think your bullies see it that way? I bet they think they're the *tzadikim* and you're the *rasha.* Who is to say you are right and they are wrong? Are you sure that *Hashem* sees it your way?

Whenever you are angry, you feel like a victim. But the people you're angry at feel that you are the bully. That's because your *nefesh habehamis* uses anger to scare them off or beat them up. So if you go around being angry with your bullies, you probably look like a *rasha.*

In fact, many victims are actually accused by schools of being bullies. Has this ever happened to you? If so, it probably made you furious because you felt it was unfair. (And your fury makes you look even more like the *real* bully).

There's an easy way to determine if people who are making you suffer feel they're your bully or your victim. Ask yourself: "Are they angry with me?" If they are, you can be sure they don't like how you are treating them — they feel that they're your victims. This is actually what goes on whenever two people are angry with each other. Each one thinks they're the *tzadik* and the other is the *rasha.*

There are people we might call "true bullies" — they have fun picking on others, but they're not angry. They're cool and confident while their victims walk around feeling angry.

There are people who are mean to others and have no friends at all. They may seem like bullies to us, but they feel like colossal victims. They are so angry with everybody for not liking them that all they want to do is take revenge. If you know people like that, they need help. (Make sure they read this book!)

It's easy to think of bullies as abnormal, evil creatures designed to hurt us and ruin our lives. The truth is they really are not different from the rest of us. They want exactly what we want: to be winners in life. We all want to be powerful. We all want respect. And we all want to be liked and admired. The difference between bullies and their victims is that the bullies are better at getting what they want. Thinking of people who upset us as *resha'im* and ourselves as *tzadikim* helps us feel better, but it doesn't solve any problems. It is much more helpful to think of people as winners and losers. When our bullies are making us miserable, we are losing and they are winning—unless, of course, we are making them miserable at the same time. Then we are both losing.

Just about everyone we call bullies are buddies to their friends. Bullies protect their buddies and enjoy being tough enough to stand up against others. If they thought of you as a friend, they would fight for you, too!

We may not want to admit it, but many of the people we think of as bullies have a trait we admire: courage. What they do may not be smart or nice, but they have the courage to challenge other people. Of course, it doesn't take much daring to pick on smaller and weaker children, but many of them stand up to those who are bigger and stronger. They are even willing to risk punishment from adults who take the side of the victims.

START THINKING OF YOUR BULLIES AS BUDDIES

To turn your bullies into buddies, you have to start thinking of them as buddies. As long as you think of them as enemies, that's what they will be. Strange as it may sound, I want you to tell yourself they are doing you a favor when they pick on you.

You may be thinking, *"Is your head on straight? They're doing me a favor? They're destroying my life!"*

I know it sounds crazy. But think for a minute about professional boxers. Boxers want to become great fighters and develop the skills to win. Do you think they will ever succeed without someone to spar against? Of course not! They need sparring partners who are willing to go into the ring and slug it out with them.

Do boxers *hate* their sparring partners? Do you think they are mad at them for hitting back and trying to knock them out? Do they wish the earth would swallow them up like Korach so they'll never be able to  hurt them again? No. They need sparring partners. Without this kind of practice, they will never become successful boxers.

The same thing is true with your bullies. Think of them as your sparring partners in the game of life, and they will help you train to be a winner. Remember, people are going to try to bully you throughout your life. The sooner you learn how to deal with them, the sooner your life as a winner will begin.

Therefore, it helps to see your bullies as your sparring partners. Be grateful to them for giving you the chance to practice your skills. If it weren't for them, you would not be reading this book and learning how to become a winner with people for the rest of your life.

Taking on your bullies may not always go smoothly. You're likely to make mistakes sometimes, especially in the beginning, but that's how life is. The professional boxer doesn't win every time. If you lose, don't become angry with your bullies. Just do your best to win the next time.

There's another reason to think of bullies as buddies. Until now they have been mean to you, so you think of them as bad. Would you feel the same way if instead of hurting you they protected you? Of course not! Your goal is to turn your bullies into buddies. When you succeed, they will indeed be good in your eyes. To start that process, all you have to do is begin thinking of them as good. The sooner you do, the quicker you'll start to win.

WHAT YOUR BULLIES WANT

Remember, the best way to influence people is by offering carrots. If you can figure out how to make your bullies feel good, they will stop making you miserable. Some of them might even become your friends.

Remember the three things your bullies want: power, respect and popularity. These are exactly the same things just about everyone wants, including you. The difference lies in how they go about getting them.

There are two ways people can have power over you. One way is by having you on their side. The other way is by having you against them but scared of them. If you are afraid of them, you lose and they are in a higher position.

When your bullies are mean to you, one way of looking at the situation is that it's their way of testing you. They want to know if you are for them or against them. They could do this by being nice to you, and you would be on their side. But if they do this, they are making the test too easy. Why *wouldn't* you be on their side if they're nice to you? So the real test is if you are on their side even if they are mean to you. If you become angry with them, you fail the test. You prove you are against them and that you deserve to be treated badly. If you tell on them and try to get them in trouble, then you have erased any doubt in their minds that you are an enemy.

On the other hand, if you don't respond with anger, you have passed your bully's test. They see that you don't hurry to consider them enemies just because they're trying to demonstrate power over you. The same thing is true when parents and *mechanchim* are mean to you. Because of their roles, they need to make you obey them. If you become angry when they try to control you, they will see you as defiant and will become tougher on you. But if you respect their authority, they will know you are on their side and will treat you better.

Your bullies want respect. Everyone does. If you become angry with them, you are disrespecting them. They will be angry in return and will try to make you suffer. However, if you give them respect they will like you. It is not necessary to do everything your bullies tell you to do, even if they are your parents and *mechanchim*. However, you do need to show them respect. Show them respect and you will be amazed by how much freedom they give you. They will actually be happier if you *disobey them respectfully* than if you *obey them disrespectfully!*

You may wonder, *What does it mean "to disobey someone respectfully" and "to obey them disrespectfully"?* Let's say you're playing chess with a friend, and your parents tell you to stop playing and do your homework instead. So you do it, but meanwhile your friend had to go home, and you didn't finish the game. You tell your parents,

"Are you *happy* now? I did my homework and now my friend is gone and we didn't finish the game! You are so mean!" Even though you obeyed them, they will not be happy with you this way. On the other hand, you can tell them, "I'd love to do my homework, but my friend has to leave soon and we're almost done with the game. I promise I'll do it as soon as the game is over." Even though you're disobeying your parents, they will like you much better this way.

The third thing your bullies want is popularity. We all do to some degree. It helps to think of popularity like a ladder. It feels good to be at the top and lousy to be at the bottom. True bullies — those who don't see themselves as victims — are usually quite popular and they get to be at the top of the ladder. They may have the unofficial role as leader. To be on top, they use both the carrot and the stick. They make their followers feel good by protecting them and making them feel "in" with the cool group. But they'll also be mean sometimes so that everyone will be afraid of them. This way people are never sure of how the leader will treat them, and will spend much of their time and energy "sucking up" to them to try to be on their good side. Girls in such a position are often referred to as queen bees. But you should avoid "sucking up" because it makes you a loser.

The truth is that to be happy, you don't need to be at the very top of the ladder. It is tough to be on top because other people will want to push you down.

But you don't want to be at the bottom of the ladder, either. The more you let other people control your feelings, thoughts and actions, the lower you put yourself on the ladder. This book will be teaching you how to have a higher position on the social ladder by getting people to like and respect you, and without being a suck-up.

THE WORST WAY TO GET POWER

Making people happy is not the only way to have power. Another way is to make them suffer. In a struggle for power, the winner is the one who comes out feeling the best and the loser is the one who feels the worst. So if you make somebody feel worse than you, you are the one with the greater power.

There are different ways to make people suffer. Some of the most common ones are:

1. Hurting their feelings
2. Hurting their bodies
3. Hurting their reputations
4. Damaging or stealing their possessions
5. Getting them in trouble
6. Threatening them

All of these methods can give you power. At the same time, they turn people into your enemies, so you also lose power. They are likely to turn their friends against you. They will also be looking for opportunities to get *nekamah* against you. Even if you are bigger and stronger than they are, they can still find ways to hurt you.

You may have recognized the ways your own bullies make you miserable. If you think honestly, you may realize you sometimes do some of these same things to others. It's a good idea to stop. You will gain friends and avoid making enemies, so your power will increase.

The only possible exception is item No. 6 — making people afraid of you. Sometimes it can be helpful to have people afraid of you. Then they'll obey you and avoid doing anything against you. But this will work only if you know how to instill fear in people. Chances are if you were such a person, you wouldn't be reading this book.

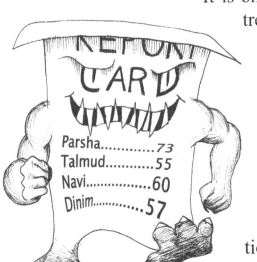

It is only safe to have people afraid of you if you also treat them like friends. That way they will feel they are following you because they *want* to make you happy, not because they're scared you'll hurt them.

If you are in a position in which you need to get people to obey you, such as *menahel*, parent, boss, *mashgiach* or police officer it may even be *necessary* to use fear. If students weren't afraid of getting lousy report cards or being sent to detention, do you think they'd work so hard in school all day long and then go home to study and do homework?

TURNING BULLIES INTO BUDDIES — THE SECRET

The reason so many of us become victims of bullying is that we make certain common mistakes. When people are mean to us, we treat them like enemies. Then they treat us back like enemies.

We just don't realize we're treating them like enemies because no one ever explained to us, "This is what it means to treat someone like an enemy." In fact, when we're making these mistakes, it feels to us like we're doing the right thing. That's because we're following our *nefesh habehamis*. If we were living in the jungle, they would probably be the right things to do. But in civilization they become the wrong things. In order to stop people from treating us badly, and even to turn them into friends, we need to recognize these mistakes and stop making them. Instead, we need to follow our *nefesh haElokis*, which wants us to live by *ve'ahavta le'reacha kamocha*. Then people become nicer to us, they like and respect us more, and we all come out being winners.

When you stop making these mistakes, you will immediately get along better not only with fellow students but also with your brothers and sisters–even with your parents!

Each mistake will be explained in detail in a section of its own. Even though these mistakes are common, they are not obvious. If they were obvious, no one would make them and bullying wouldn't be a problem. In fact, some of the mistakes are things that most people think are the *right* things to do about bullying!

Mistake 1: Getting angry
Mistake 2: Being afraid
Mistake 3: Retaliating
Mistake 4: Defending ourselves
Mistake 5: Telling on bullies

MISTAKE 1: GETTING ANGRY

This mistake is the most common reason we get bullied, and that is why it is listed first.

The Torah teaches us how important it is to control our anger. Mishlei 16:32 says, "He that is slow to anger is better than the mighty."

The Gemora, in Pesachim 66b, says, "Anger will cause a *chacham* to lose his wisdom, a person who is destined for greatness to forfeit it."

The Rambam considered anger to be the greatest sin. He said, "When someone becomes angry it is as though he worshipped idols."

You may think that it is extremely hard to control your anger. To make it easier, I will ask you a few questions.

Questions: Is anger a friendly feeling?

Answer: Anger is a hostile feeling. We only get angry with people when they act *against* us. *Hashem* designed our *nefesh habehamis* to get angry in order to help us survive in the lawless jungle, where there would be real enemies trying to hurt or kill us. It responds with anger when we are threatened or attacked, so that we'll scare off the enemy. If the enemy isn't scared, we need to have the drive to tear it to pieces before it tears us to pieces.

So if I get angry with you, I am not being nice to you. I am treating you like you're my enemy. Even if you're a good friend, at the moment I'm angry with you I feel you're doing something against me. Then your *nefesh habehamis* will feel under attack by me and will get angry back. Now we are treating each other like enemies!

Question: When you get angry, who is the loser?

Answer: You are. To defeat you, people don't have to break your bones or make you bleed. All they have to do is get you angry. When you're angry, you feel miserable and they feel powerful. Since their *nefesh habehamis* enjoys winning, they will keep on doing exactly what gets you angry.

Questions: When someone is mean to you and you get angry, who makes you angry?

Answer: You do!

Of course it doesn't feel that way. When you get angry, do you decide to get angry? Do you tell yourself, *"I think getting angry is the smart thing to do in this situation because it will help me win"?* Of course not! Since you get angry without deciding to, it feels like others make you angry.

It's not just you. Everyone is like that. Whenever we get angry with people, it feels like they have a remote control to our brain and they're pressing the "anger button." Why? It's because of our *nefesh habehamis*. Remember that it is programmed to help animals survive and win in the lawless world of the jungle.

In the jungle, getting angry is the first step to winning a conflict. If you attack me, I need to get angry as quickly as possible in order to scare you off or defeat you in battle. Since my *nefesh habehamis* gets angry in a split second, without my having to think about it, it feels like you made me angry. But I really did it to myself.

However, we don't live in the jungle. We live in civilization, where life is much safer. We don't have to hunt for food or fight physically to survive. In fact, there are very strict laws against fighting, so there is a good chance that fighting will get us in deep trouble. I may want to punch you in the nose, but I am not allowed to. You can do all kinds of things to get me mad without being afraid that I will hurt you. You can laugh while I get angrier and angrier. The angrier I get, the more I become the loser.

In civilization, we should listen to our *nefesh haElokis*, which tells us to control our anger. This way we won't turn people into enemies, and we will both be winners.

You may be thinking, *"But how can I just decide to stop becoming angry when people are mean to me?"*

Do you remember the Verbal Bullying Experiment? I hope you tried it with at least a couple of people. You asked the subject to insult you two separate times. The first time, you got angry. The second time, you didn't. Even though the experiment was make-believe, it works the same way in real life. *Hashem* gave you *bechirah chofshis*. It is your choice whether or not you get angry.

Your goal is to be a winner, so disable the "anger button" in your brain. Show your bullies they can try all they want, but they can't get you angry! This is really not so hard to do once you realize it. There are many things our bodies do without our awareness but we can still control them. When you see something funny, your automatic response is to laugh, but you can easily stop yourself. If a doctor tests your reflexes by tapping below your knee with a hammer, your leg will automatically respond by kicking, but you can decide not to let your leg kick. And when people are mean to you, the natural response is to get angry, but you can decide not to.

When you refuse to become angry, your bullies will discover they can no longer defeat you. They will feel like fools and losers every time they pick on you. Before long, they won't even *try* to get you upset because they don't want to lose. You will become the winner without doing anything against them.

Another strange thing will happen. Your bullies will start liking you better when they see they can't defeat you. Why? For three basic reasons:

1. *You are no longer angry with them.* People don't like you when you are angry.
2. *They can respect you now.* People want to have friends they can respect. If they can get you angry, you look like a loser. But when they can no longer defeat you, they will respect you more and will feel more comfortable having you as a friend.
3. *You are showing them respect.* Your bullies enjoy respect just as much as you do. Anger is not respectful. When you are no longer reacting with anger, you are being more respectful, so they will like you better!

MISTAKE 2: BEING AFRAID

"What do you mean—I shouldn't be afraid of my bullies? They are scary! They ridicule me in front of everyone! They hurt my feelings. They threaten me, push me around and hit me! Of course I should be afraid of them!"

You were probably able to realize that you can decide to control your anger. But how about fear? How can you just decide not to be scared?

I will try to help you by teaching you to use your big brain and your *nefesh haElokis*.

Are you afraid of other children? If so, what are they doing to scare you? Are they hitting you over the head with a baseball bat every time they see you? Are they stabbing you with a knife? Are they throwing you down the stairs and so that you get terribly bruised and perhaps even have your bones broken? If so, of course you should be afraid of them. But don't even think of this as bullying. It is criminal behavior and you should get the police involved against them. They need to be punished terribly and sent to a school or institution for violent or disturbed people.

Chances are, though, that this is not what's happening to you. You are probably afraid of them because they do things that mostly hurt your feelings, like insult you, talk about you behind your back, bring you mean rumors and tell you that you can't sit with them at the lunch table or come to their parties. They may also being doing physical things that are annoying and even causing a little pain, like poke you with a pencil, bump into you when they pass you in the hallway, knock your books out of your hands or throw your yarmulke around. They may even tell you that they are going to beat you up after school, but they never do it. Maybe they playfight with you, and you don't like it, but they aren't hitting you so hard that you have to go to the school nurse or to the hospital.

Though these things are not as terrible as crimes, they can still bother you so much that you are afraid of going to school.

Fortunately, you can learn not to be afraid, especially if the children who are scaring you aren't injuring your body.

First, ask yourself, "Are the children that I am afraid of angry with me?" Angry people can become dangerous. As you learned a little earlier, people get angry when they feel that someone did something wrong to them. Then they want revenge, so they may do something much worse in response. So if some-

one is angry with you, it's because they feel *you* are *their* bully. Ask them why they are mad at you, and see if you can work out the problem. And make sure to apologize for hurting them. Then you won't have to be afraid of them.

Probably the most common reason that children in school are angry with others is that they tell on them to the teachers, *rebbeim* or *menahel.* If you're constantly telling on your fellow *talmidim,* don't be surprised that they are mean to you. You need to stop doing that, but we'll talk more about that in another lesson.

Almost all of your fears are unnecessary. The reason you are afraid is because you don't know how to deal with the difficult situations. Let's say no one ever taught you that water can put out fire. One day a fire starts in a wastebasket in your kitchen and no one else is home. Will you be scared? You'll be *terrified!* The fire can grow right in front of your eyes. The whole house might burn down while you're watching.

But let's say you learned that water can put out fire. How scared will you be? Not very. You'll quickly go to the sink and get some water to throw on the fire.

The same thing is true with your bullies. If you are afraid of them, it's because you don't know how to stop them from making you suffer. But once you are done reading this book, you will know how to handle almost any bullying situation, so you won't feel so afraid. In fact, you are going to treat people so well that they will probably want to help you, not hurt you.

Now I will explain to you something you might find hard to believe. The fact that you are afraid of your bullies actually makes them continue doing the things you are afraid of! To help you understand this, I want to ask you a couple of questions about the nature of fear.

Question: Are we afraid of friends or enemies?

Answer: Enemies, of course. Friends don't want to hurt us, so there's no need to fear them. Therefore, by being afraid of people, we are treating them like enemies. So they'll probably treat us back like enemies.

Question: When we are afraid of someone, who is in the stronger position?

Answer: They are. So by being afraid, we put ourselves in the weaker position. We automatically lose, and losers don't get respect. Since winning feels good, our bullies will continue doing whatever keeps us afraid of them.

"But how can I just stop being afraid? The bullies are dangerous and can hurt me."

You can do it by understanding how the *nefesh habehamis* works. *Hashem* programmed it to feel fear when we are in real danger so that we will run away and prevent ourselves from getting hurt.

If we were taking a hike in the middle of the jungle, or in a war zone in which there's shooting and bombing going on all around us, fear would be necessary for survival. It would help keep us away from animals or soldiers that might kill us. But in our normal lives, including in school, we are not allowed to injure each other and everyone knows it. The law is like an invisible shield protecting us. Our bullies realize we can get them in serious trouble if they hurt us, and they'll lose big time.

However, to win, they don't need to injure us. They can use our *nefesh habehamis* against us. All they need to do is quickly raise their arm as though to hit us, or to say threatening words. Then our *nefesh habehamis* reacts with fear as though they are actually intending to injure us. When we get scared, they feel powerful and automatically win. Since being powerful and winning feel good, they will continue doing the same things that scare you.

But you want to win and to get respect. The way to do this is listen to your *nefesh haElokis*, which wants you to love your fellow Jew, and to your brain, which tells you that the kids are not really looking to hurt you, so you have nothing to be afraid of.

Even if the kids who are scaring you are bigger and stronger than you, don't worry. You aren't in real danger. Most of them are not the evil villains you have been imagining them to be. They are just playing around with you. When you stop being afraid of them, they feel foolish trying to scare you, and they soon stop. Then they cease being your enemies and become free to be your friends. In fact, if you are small, and a big *bochur* knocks into you in the hallway whenever he passes you, it could be that he likes you and wants to be your friend. You can't expect him to hug you, but he'll knock into you. If you are scared and avoid him, you'll never become friends. But if you don't avoid him, and instead say something like, "Hey, Moish, nice bumping into you again!" a friendship has a chance to develop. Friendship has nothing to do with size. Just because someone is twice your size, it doesn't mean that he can't be your friend.

So when you find your body telling you, *"Oh, no, the bullies are so big and strong! I'm afraid they are going to hurt me,"* catch yourself and realize that this fear makes you automatically lose. Instead, tell yourself:

"They are bigger and stronger than me, but I don't have to be afraid of them because they aren't going to injure me. They don't hate me enough to want to hurt me, and they don't want to get into serious trouble, either. They just want to enjoy the power of scaring me. So they can act as scary as they want, and it doesn't bother me in the least!"

With this attitude, you will always be a winner. You will discover that people like and respect you, no matter how small or weak you may be. In fact, if you have no fear, they may even admire you and want to act as your protectors, *especially* if you are small and weak! So stop being afraid of them, and you just might get yourself some free bodyguards!

So far, I've been talking mostly about people making us afraid they will hurt us physically. However, that is not the only way people can have power over us. Another simple way is by getting us to fear what they *think* of us. We want their approval, and we're terrified they will reject us, that they won't want to be our friends. While everyone can have this kind of fear, it is more common among girls. Boys are more likely to scare others physically. Girls are more likely to scare others with rejection.

The origin of this fear is also in our *nefesh habehamis*. In the jungle, there are no homeless shelters or Welfare Department to take care of us. Members of a tribe need to cooperate with each other in order to survive. What the rest of the tribe thought of us was very important. If they didn't approve of us, they would put us in *cherem*. They would act like we didn't exist, and we'd be all alone. After a while, we would get sick and maybe even die. You may be aware that even Jewish communities throughout history often used *cherem* as punishment for individuals who did something terrible. *Cherem* could be a punishment almost as bad as death.

However, in modern life we don't live in such danger. No matter what our friends think of us, our parents will love us, we will to have food to eat, a bed to sleep in, schools to learn in, and hospitals to take care of us when we are sick. Our basic survival doesn't depend on what people think of us. Our *nefesh habehamis*, though, doesn't know this and reacts as though we're living in the lawless world of the jungle.

Today, when we care too much what people think of us, we are giving them power over us for nothing. Think of it this way: If I care about what you think of *me,* but you don't care what I think of *you,* who is in a stronger position? You are! I will be trying to act or dress in a way I hope you will approve of, while you are doing absolutely nothing for me. You are the one in control. It's like I'm making you my boss. I become the big loser, and losers don't get respect.

Think about the really famous, successful, or powerful people in the world. Do they care what we personally think about them? No. They live their lives the way they want. They will only do what it takes to get people to buy their products or services or, if they're politicians, to vote for them. Many celebrities will purposely behave or dress outrageously. They know people will be so impressed by their daring and originality that they will want to be like them and spend money on their performances or products.

If you want to be happy and successful, stop worrying that others will think badly of you. Follow your *nefesh haElokis,* which guides you to live the way *Hashem* wants. To win the approval game that people play with you, tell yourself:

"People can think whatever they want about me, and it's perfectly OK. I don't mind if they think I'm ugly, stupid, fat, nerdy or weird. No one is perfect, and I don't have to change to get people's approval. This is my life, and I'm going to live it according to what I believe a good Jew should do."

You will discover that the less you worry what others think of you, the happier and more powerful you become. People will actually like and respect you more when they can't control you, and you live by your own values rather than by theirs—as long as you are not hurting them, of course.

There's another thing you should understand about children who make fun of you.

Since they are making fun of your imperfections or differences, it seems like they hate you for being different and would love it if you were just like them.

But it only *seems* that way. The truth is they are happy you are different. Part of us wants to be the same as everyone else so that we won't stick out and be made fun of. But deep down, another part of us wants to be different from everyone so that we can feel special. If you were just like your bullies, that wouldn't please them! You would be preventing them from feeling special. And you wouldn't like it, either, because you wouldn't be special.

If people were all the same, life would be horribly boring. Even more importantly, the world couldn't function if everyone were the same. You need people with different abilities and characteristics to do all the different jobs that are required to keep society running. So feel different, and feel special. Love others for being different from you, and they will love you for being different from them.

By the way, did you ever hear the expression, "Opposites attract"? Well, there's a lot of truth to that. In fact, the kids who tease you may be drawn to you because they are attracted by your difference. You just can't see it because they are trying to make themselves feel good by making fun of you. So don't fall into the trap of getting upset when they make fun of your differences, and after a while they will stop. Maybe they'll end up being your friends because they find your differences so interesting!

MISTAKE 3: RETALIATING

To retaliate means to attack someone back, to get revenge against them for having attacked us first.

Question: Do we retaliate against friends or enemies?

Answer: Retaliation, by definition, is what we do to enemies. An enemy attacks us, and then we attack them back. Even though they started, when we retaliate, we are treating them like enemies, so they feel justified attacking us again.

It is natural for us to want to retaliate against those who attack us first. This is the reaction of our *nefesh habehamis*. That's because in the jungle, if an enemy attacks us and we can't escape, it becomes necessary to attack back. The alternative may be death. Retaliation is also often necessary in warfare. If another country attacks us because they decided to wipe us out, we may get destroyed if we don't retaliate.

But that's not the situation in our regular lives. It is against the law to hurt others. Our bullies know this. Unless we have given them a really good reason to hate us, they are not trying to send us to the hospital. We don't need to retaliate in order to win because we are not in real danger. If we attack them in return, they will probably want to attack us again even harder.

To be honest, this is not always true. It is possible that if we retaliate, they will become scared of us and decide not to mess with us. But when this works, we only have to do it once. If we find that we are constantly retaliating, and our bullies continue attacking, the retaliation is not working and is probably making the situation worse. Someone might even end up getting seriously hurt.

You should assume that your bullies are not stupid. They don't want to get in trouble. They want *you* to get in trouble, so they do a clever trick by using your *nefesh habe-*

hamis against you. They push or hit you quietly when the *mechanech* isn't looking. They hope you will get angry and attack them back so loudly that everyone notices you. They started but you are the one who ends up getting punished! By attacking back, instead of becoming a winner, you become a king-sized loser.

I hope you have already tried the Physical Bullying Experiment with at least a few people and found out how nicely it works. It is hard for someone to keep on attacking you if you are doing nothing back. Even though it seems like you are "letting the bullies get away with it," you are really defeating them. They feel foolish attacking someone who isn't fighting back. It also makes you look tough because you can take a push or a hit and it doesn't upset you.

There is another important principle that I want you to learn from this. Everyone thinks that in a fight, the *first* person to hit is the one who started the fight. The truth is that the *second* person to hit really started the fight! Does this sound *meshuggeh?* But it's not. It takes two people to make a fight. When someone hits you, there is no fight yet. As you discovered in the experiment, if you do nothing back, no fight happens. It's only when you attack back that a fight erupts! So yes, even though you are the second person to hit, you actually are the one who started the fight.

Warning: *This rule does not apply if you are facing someone who is intent on injuring you no matter what you do, and you are backed in a corner with no one to rescue you. If attacking back is your only chance for preventing serious harm to yourself, of course you must do it. Please remember, though, that this is an extremely rare situation that might never happen to you. If people are truly looking to injure you, they're either criminals, or you must have given them a mighty good reason for hating you — like telling on them and getting them in trouble!*

MISTAKE 4: DEFENDING YOURSELF

This might be the hardest idea to accept in the entire book. It may make sense to you that attacking bullies is wrong, but why shouldn't you *defend* yourself from them? Are you to simply let them treat you like a *shmatteh?*

Question: Do we defend ourselves from friends or enemies?

Answer: Obviously, we defend ourselves from enemies. We don't need to defend ourselves from friends because friends don't want to hurt us.

Therefore, if we defend ourselves from people, it means that we consider them enemies. So we can't expect them to be friendly.

Question: If one person is attacking and the other is defending, who is in the stronger position?

Answer: The attacker is in the stronger position. By defending ourselves – especially from words – we put the attacker on top and ourselves at the bottom. The harder we defend ourselves, the bigger we lose, and the attacker will continue attacking to keep us in the losing defensive position.

If you don't want to be the loser and you don't want to have enemies, you must decide not to defend yourself when someone attacks you. You will get more respect because you will not be the loser. Your bullies will like you better because you'll be treating them like friends rather than enemies.

But won't you get hurt if you don't defend yourself?

Not if the attacks are verbal attacks, with words, as most attacks are. Words don't break our bones or make us bleed.

You also don't need to defend yourself from physical actions that are just meant to scare you, not to hurt you. If you defend yourself, you are more likely to get hurt because you are now treating the person like an enemy, and you are also putting him in the stronger position, so he will escalate his attack. And that's when you might get hurt.

But if the attacker is actually trying to hurt you physically, say, by punching you hard or hitting you with a stick or a rock, of course you must defend yourself. Later in this book you will learn more about handling dangerous situations.

It takes two people to make a fight. When you don't defend yourself, there's no fight. Your bullies are likely to feel foolish attacking you if you aren't defending yourself, so they'll quickly stop trying. And then there will be no need to defend yourself.

MISTAKE 5: TELLING ON YOUR BULLIES

Have adults been urging you to tell them when other kids bully you? Have they been teaching you, "Telling is not tattling"?

Please be careful about following such advice. One of the best ways to make people despise you is by informing on them to the authorities. This is true whether you are telling your *rebbe* on other students, your parents on your brother or sister, your boss on a co-worker, or the police on your neighbor. The harder your bullies get punished, the more intensely they are going to hate you. And they will be burning to get back at you, either by hurting you again or by getting *you* in trouble.

This is what happened between Yosef and his brothers. Yosef would inform on his brothers to their father, Yaacov Avinu, and as a result they planned to do away with him altogether. Yiddishkeit does not respect informers, and we even have *brachos* against them.

If it is usually a mistake to tell on bullies, why are adults saying you must do it? It's because they care about you and want to help you. They want to be your heroes fighting off your evil bullies. They just don't realize that their efforts to help may not work. In fact, when adults try to help children in their conflicts with each other, the fighting almost always gets worse. Since both children want the adults on their side, they each argue even harder to convince the adults they are right and their opponent is wrong.

If you have ever told your parents or *mechanchim* on your siblings or schoolmates, you probably discovered that it doesn't help. It may feel good to have the adult on your side, but the problem continues. Maybe your bullies leave you alone for a short while after they get yelled at or punished, but before long they're picking on you again. And as long as you tell on *them*, they'll look for opportunities to tell on *you*.

When confronted by adults, do your bullies simply say, "Oh, yes, I'm guilty. I'm so sorry. I won't do it again"? Sometimes they do. But more often they start blaming you and trying to get you in trouble. If the adults are attempting to be fair, there is a good chance they will decide that you are the guilty one. And if your bullies are popular, more children will testify in their favor than in yours. This makes you look like the real bully. You end up in trouble and being the big loser.

Do you like it when your brother or sister tells your parents on you? Of course not! Your parents are the most important people in the world to you. You want them to love you and be on your side. When your siblings get you in trouble with your parents, you become angry with your siblings *and* your parents.

It's the same thing in school. The teacher is the most important person in your school day. The last thing you want is for other *talmidim* to get the teacher against you.

Well, your bullies are no different from you. When you tell on them, they'd like to see you get struck by lightning. So remember: *mah shesanu ailecha al ta'aseh lachavercha.* If you hate it when people tell on you, you shouldn't tell on them, either.

Do you want respect? Do you want to be a winner? Of course you do. Well, no one gets the admiration of classmates by telling the teacher on other students. When you tell on your bullies, you are letting everyone know that you can't handle them by yourself. You are declaring that you are weaker than they are, that they are defeating you, and that you need a grown-up's help to win. Even if you get your bullies punished, you still lose because everyone knows you didn't defeat them by yourself. Even the teachers who help you won't truly respect you. They would admire you much more if you solved your bully problem on your own. In fact, people will respect you more if you deal with your bullies by yourself and *lose* than if you get an adult to defeat them for you. So, when you tell on your bullies you look like a loser, and losers don't get respect.

Very often people tell on each other. It could be that you tell on your bullies, and they tell on you. It goes back and forth and the telling never ends. Should you stop telling on them? Certainly. Let them tell on you all they want, but don't tell on them. And don't get angry or defensive when they tell on you, either. When the adult confronts you, calmly and sincerely apologize for what you are accused of. Even if you didn't do it, don't say, "I promise, I didn't do it!" You can simply say, "I'm sorry. I don't remember doing it, but I hope [the kid who complained] is okay." After a while, kids will feel childish telling on you if you never tell on them, and will stop. If for some strange reason they continue telling on you, the adults will have more respect for you than for them. *They* will look like the bad or immature ones, not you.

There are only a few instances when you should tell adults on other kids. One is if you are asking for advice. It is always okay to go to an adult you respect, saying, "I am having trouble with some of the other *talmidim*. Can you please give me advice on how to deal with them." Be sure to make it clear that you don't want the adult to reprimand or punish them. You only want their advice on what *you* should do.

If you see a student who is a loner, looks unhappy, or gets picked on a lot, they very well may need help. Aside from the misery they may be experiencing regularly, they may be in danger of hurting themselves or others. If you aren't sure they are already going for appropriate help, talk to a school counselor, *mechanech* or *rebbe* about them. That act may end up doing a great deal of good for them.

You should tell adults when someone has committed a crime, or to *prevent* them from committing a crime. A crime means something that actually causes harm to people's bodies or possessions or denies them the freedoms granted by the government.

This means that no one is allowed to make you bleed or break your bones. For this they should be punished so they won't want to do it again. They are not allowed to destroy or steal your possessions. If they do, and are not willing to pay you back or return the items, then you should tell the authorities. If kids make up lies about you so that you'll get kicked out of school, they should be punished. People are not allowed to prevent you from enjoying the rights everyone else enjoys, for instance, by getting you fired from your job or ruining your chance to get a good *shidduch*. If you have good reason to believe that someone is going to harm someone else, then it may be necessary to tell the authorities so they can step in to stop them in time.

But don't try to get others in trouble for hurting your feelings. That is not a crime. Whether your feelings are hurt depends upon you, not them, so it is wrong to get them punished. Don't tell on them if they call you names, gossip about you, or shove you without harming you. (In later chapters you will learn how to handle these situations effectively).

But there is someone you *should* tell if your bully does something you don't like. Who? Your bully! Think of it this way. Let's say you hurt me. When will you like me better—if I tell the authorities, or if I tell *you?* Of course you would prefer that I tell you instead of trying to get you in trouble. You will respect me more for having the courage and decency to talk to you directly, and you will like me better for not trying to get you in trouble. You are much more likely to apologize and stop bothering me if I tell *you* than if I tell your *morah,* parent, or a policeman. Well, your bullies are just like you. If you need to tell someone, tell the person who's bothering you, not the authorities. Just be sure that when you talk to your bully, you are not angry or threatening. Talk the way you would to a good friend. I can't guarantee that your bullies will always listen to you, but you can be sure you that the results will be better if you tell *them* than if you tell *on* them.

THREE WARNINGS

When you begin following the advice for getting your bullies to stop picking on you, you need to know what to expect or you may fall into traps that will make the bullying continue.

1. The bullying will get worse before it gets better.

Wouldn't it be wonderful if all you had to do is read this book and then you would never be picked on again? Well, it's almost that simple, but not quite. In fact, you must be prepared for the bullying to get *worse* before it gets better. But only for a couple of days.

When you change your attitude, your bullies will discover you aren't getting upset. They'll feel confused. They'll think something is terribly wrong with you. Maybe you went blind and don't see them. Maybe you went deaf and don't hear them. They won't like the sensation that they aren't winning. But they really *want* to upset you, so they will probably try even harder. They figure if they bother you long enough, eventually they'll get to you.

After a while, they'll become tired of feeling foolish and will stop bothering you. A little later they will try again, hoping you are back to your old self and will get upset. Again, it won't work.

So when you see the harassment intensifying, don't think, *"Oh, no, this isn't working! The bullying is only getting worse!"* It is working. It's just that your bullies have been winning against you for a long time, and they want to continue winning. Plus, you have been letting them know all along that the bullying bothers you, and they need some time to figure out that it doesn't anymore.

2. You must follow these instructions all the time.

The only way to succeed in stopping your tormentors is to follow the instructions in this book — all the time. If your bullies discover that you get upset once in awhile, they will know their bullying really does bother you; they just have to try harder and more often. So the abuse won't stop. It may even get worse. Only when your bullies find they can never upset you will they stop trying to upset you.

3. Bullying won't completely disappear.

Follow the instructions in this book and your situation will improve dramatically. But don't expect to never get picked on again in your life. Everyone gets picked on once in a while, and there's nothing in the world we can do to change that. The difference is that it will happen much less often than it used to, and the same individual won't bother you more than once in a long while. Most importantly, it won't upset you when you're picked on. In fact, sometimes you may even find it funny.

Section Two Quiz

1. The Golden Rule means that:
    a. You should own more gold than other people.
    b. You should only be nice to people when they are nice to you.
    c. You should be nice to people even when they are mean to you.
    d. People should be punished when they are mean to you.

2. To stop being a victim, it is important to start thinking of bullies as:
    a. People just like us.
    b. Bad guys.
    c. Idiots.
    d. Just jealous.

3. When you get angry, you feel:
    a. Like a bully but look like a victim.
    b. Stupid but look smart.
    c. Like a victim but look like a bully.
    d. Smart and look smart.

4. The way to grow up tough and strong is to:
    a. Never experience any hardship.
    b. Have adults protect you from mean kids.
    c. **a** and **b**
    d. Have experience dealing with hardship.

5. Parents and teachers will like you better when you:
    a. Disobey them respectfully.
    b. Obey them rudely.
    c. Tell them they are unfair.
    d. Disobey them rudely.

6. If you want kids to stop being your enemies, you should:
    a. Warn them you'll get them in trouble if they are mean to you.
    b. Treat them the way they treat you.
    c. Give them whatever they want.
    d. Show them respect.

7. Anger is the emotion you feel toward:
    a. An enemy.
    b. A friend.
    c. Food.
    d. Clothing.

8. To prevent anger, you should adopt the attitude that:
    a. "No one has a right to be mean to me."
    b. "Life has to be fair."
    c. "I must never be a loser."
    d. "People do have a right to be mean to me."

9. Getting angry will make people:
    a. Like you.
    b. Respect you.
    c. Be angry back at you.
    d. Want to give you what you want.

10. When people call you stupid, you should:
    a. Call them stupid back.
    b. Tell the teacher.
    c. Tell them you aren't stupid.
    d. Be grateful to them for encouraging you to be smarter.

11. If you are afraid of people, you are treating them like:
    a. Enemies.
    b. Friends.
    c. Cousins.
    d. Teachers.

12. You shouldn't fear bullies because:
    a. They only want to scare you.
    b. They probably aren't looking to hurt you.
    c. They don't want to get in trouble.
    d. All of the above.

13. To get the most respect from people, you must:
    a. Do what's right without worrying what they think of you.
    b. Try hard to get their approval.
    c. Be afraid of what they'll think of you.
    d. Tell on them when they do something you don't like.

14. If everyone were the same:
    a. People would be happier.
    b. Life would be more fun.
    c. We couldn't feel special.
    d. We would all be nicer to each other.

15. A kid pushes you when the *rebbe* isn't looking. You get mad and push back, saying, "Get your hands off of me!" Who is most likely to get in trouble?
    a. The kid who pushed you.
    b. Both of you.
    c. The *rebbe*.
    d. You.

16. If someone is looking to hurt you no matter what you do, you should:
    a. Let them hurt you.
    b. Defend yourself or get help.
    c. Cry.
    d. Spit on them.

17. If people criticize you and you defend yourself, you are:
    a. Treating them like friends.
    b. Being nice to them.
    c. Sounding smart.
    d. Treating them like enemies.

18. When there is an attacker and a defender, the defender is in the:
    a. Weaker position.
    b. Stronger position.
    c. More enjoyable position.
    d. Smarter position.

19. Telling the *mechanchim* or *menahel* when kids bother you is a good way to:
   a. Get lots of friends.
   b. Get respect of other kids.
   c. Make kids hate you.
   d. Look mature.

20. Telling on other kids is a good idea when they:
   a. Make fun of you.
   b. Have injured someone or are about to injure someone.
   c. Throw a paper ball at you.
   d. Insult your mother.

21. If you hurt me, you will respect me most when I:
   a. Tell you that you hurt me.
   b. Tell the teacher that you hurt me.
   c. Tell your parents that you hurt me.
   d. Tell my parents that you hurt me.

22. When you get mad at people for hurting you, they are most likely to:
   a. Apologize for hurting you.
   b. Want to buy you a present.
   c. Get mad back at you.
   d. Think you are cool.

23. Most of your bullies:
   a. Are heartless *resha'im*.
   b. Want to send people to the hospital.
   c. Like to kill defenseless animals.
   d. Would feel bad if they actually broke someone's bones.

24. When you stop getting mad at your bullies, they:
   a. Will immediately thank you for being so nice.
   b. Might treat you worse for the first couple of days.
   c. Will immediately think you have changed.
   d. Will immediately feel sorry for having bothered you.

25. To stop being a victim of bullies, you have to refuse to get mad at them:
a. None of the time.
b. Some of the time.
c. Most of the time.
d. All of the time.

26. If you always follow the advice in this book:
a. You will never, ever be picked on again.
b. You will be picked on every day.
c. People will hate you.
d. You will still get picked on once in a while.

SECTION THREE:

SOME GOOD ADVICE

TREAT INSULTS AND CRITICISMS AS FRIENDLY ADVICE

Weird as it may sound, this is a wonderful and powerful rule for good relationships. If you want people to be your friends, you need to treat them like friends. This means that when people are saying negative things to you, no matter how nasty or angry they sound, it's their way of trying to get you to be a better person. Remember, our Torah teaches us to judge people favorably. So we must assume that they have good reasons for insulting and criticizing us, and we should appreciate them for it.

The last Lubavitcher Rebbe, Menachem Mendel Schneerson Z"L, said, "Love criticism. It will bring you to your highest level."

It's not natural to enjoy being criticized. Our *nefesh habehamis* experiences it as an attack. So we get angry and treat the person like an enemy.

But our *nefesh haElokis* wants us to improve, to become like *Hashem*. While it might be nice to have people treat us as though we're already perfect, no one is. People see what's wrong with us better than we do. How are we going to be able to fix our imperfections if no one lets us know what they are?

The Torah says, *hoche'ach toche'ach es amisechah velo tisa alav chet*. We are supposed to reprimand our friends when they do something wrong so they won't sin. This means not only that we're supposed to tell other people what *they're* doing wrong, they're supposed to tell us what *we're* doing wrong!

In other words, if people are going to be good Jews, they are going to criticize us. Sometimes they might not be such good Yidden and will even insult us!

It's silly to get angry when people criticize or insult us. We come out looking like losers, so they're likely to continue criticizing and insulting us. The smart thing is to do what the *nefesh haElokis* wants, and that is to be grateful to people for taking the time and effort to tell us what is wrong with us so we can try to improve.

It doesn't matter if what they are saying is wrong, or even if they aren't intending to help you. Maybe they are just looking to have fun upsetting you. It's still a mistake to get upset. Treat them as though their intentions are good, and you will automatically win.

So if someone calls you stupid, tell yourself they are saying it not because they want to hurt your feelings but because they are pressuring you to be smarter. Or if they call you a fatso, it is because they are trying to encourage you to get in shape. So why should you be upset with them?

If your parents call you a spoiled brat, don't get angry. Thank them for trying to get you to act more maturely, and then they'll be happier to give you more of what you want.

Appreciating what people tell you doesn't mean that you have to obey them – only that you should be grateful for what they say.

For example, if people urge you to shoplift, don't do it just because you're considering them to be friendly. Tell yourself they are trying to help you have things you can't afford, but you can't follow their advice because stealing is a serious *aveirah*.

Or if someone tells you to jump off a tall building, of course you shouldn't do it. But you can tell yourself they must have a very good reason for saying it. Maybe it's their way of telling you that you are acting like a *schmendrik* and you should cut it out.

Don't forget that your goal is to have people be your friends rather than enemies. If you *think* of people as your friends, they are more likely to *be* your friends.

SHOW YOU ARE HURT, NOT ANGRY

So far, you've been learning that getting angry when people are mean to us is usually a mistake. It turns us into losers, and makes them want to treat us badly again.

But what should we do about the pain? When we get angry, it is because we are being hurt in some way. Are we supposed to ignore the pain and just let people continue hurting us?

No! We should not ignore pain.

Let's understand what happens with people who hurt us repeatedly. We get angry because we want them to apologize and promise they will never do it again. Instead they get angry back, and before long they're doing the same hurtful things again. Why? It's because of what you learned in Section Two: *When you are angry, you feel like a victim but look like a bully.*

Ask yourself, *"What feeling am I showing them when I get angry?"* Anger, of course! So what will they feel in response? Anger! Do we want them to be angry with us when they hurt us? No. We want them to be *sorry*. So when we get angry, we get the opposite of what we want. Instead of feeling sorry and apologizing, they get angry back at us, as though we should feel sorry for hurting *them!*

Why do we make this common mistake? It's because of our *nefesh habehamis*. If we live in the jungle and you hurt me, you're probably doing it intentionally. Maybe you're trying to beat me up and take over my leadership of our group. Or maybe you're a wild animal trying to eat me for breakfast. I need to get angry in order to scare you off, and to have the drive to tear you to pieces before you tear *me* to pieces. Therefore, to protect us, our *nefesh habehamis* responds with anger whenever someone hurts us.

But we now live in civilization. The Torah forbids you from injuring me, and I can take you to a *beis din* if you do. If you hurt me, it's not because you are looking to eat me for breakfast. In fact, you may have hurt me unintentionally. Today, if I follow my *nefesh habehamis* and get angry, I am likely to accomplish the opposite of what I want: you get angry back and want to hurt me again.

But let's say you hurt me, and instead of getting angry, I sincerely let you know that you hurt me. How will you probably feel? Sorry! You'll probably even apologize. And that's exactly what I want.

So from now on, if someone hurts you, don't make the mistake of getting angry. Just let them know maturely how they hurt you. Will it always get you the apology you want? Not always. But you may be pleasantly surprised to discover how often you do.

DON'T BE A SORE LOSER

Wouldn't it be great if you could always be a winner in life? Unfortunately, it's impossible. Earlier in the book, I explained that life is like a game. No one wins all the time. Sometimes you win and sometimes you lose. The good news is that if you understand the advice in this chapter, you'll be a winner even when you lose.

Winning feels good and losing feels bad. That's how it has to be. *Hashem* made us that way because He wants us to be as successful as possible. But no matter how terrific we are, there are going to be people who are better than us in some ways. We have to learn to live with losing even though losing isn't fun. In fact, it's more important to learn how to deal with losing than with winning. Anyone can handle winning; it feels good. Losing is the hard part.

It is not only in games or sports that we can be losers. We can lose in all types of life situations. We can feel like losers when other children earn higher test scores, when our parents don't give us what we want, when other people win prizes, and when children tease or bully us and make us look like fools.

Many children are only happy when they win, and act as if the world is coming to an end when they lose. They scream or argue or cry. Do you act like this? Unfortunately, it only makes people lose respect for you, so they won't want to be your friends or play with you again.

People who can't stand losing often hold grudges. They can't forget or forgive. They treat the person who defeated them as though they are an eternal enemy, so they stay angry forever. When we are angry, our body actually produces chemicals that hurt us. When we hold grudges, we want to hurt the person who hurt us, but the people we are harming the most are ourselves. There is a popular saying: *Anger is like swallowing poison and hoping the other person will get sick.*

So how can you stop yourself from being a sore loser? By doing the following:

1. Realize that you can't always be the winner and there is nothing terrible about losing. Games are fun to play even when you lose. Of course winning is better, but you can't have the opportunity of winning if you don't also have the chance of losing.

2. Understand that no one is going to hate you if you lose. Do you hate people who lose against you? Of course not! It makes you happy that they lost and you won. Well, the same thing is true about others. In fact, people are more likely to be upset if you win against them, so don't worry how they'll feel about you if you lose. If you are playing on a team, it is possible that your teammates will be angry with you if you play badly and cause the team to lose. But as long as you play your best and maturely admit your errors by saying something like, "Yes, I'm really sorry I messed up," they won't stay angry with you for long.

3. Congratulate your opponents when they defeat you. This is called "being a good sport," and is the opposite of being a sore loser. Even when you lose, if you say, "*Yasher ko'ach*! You were great!" you will come out a winner. People will respect you and like you for your mature and gracious behavior, and they will be happy to play with you again.

Think about it. Let's say you defeat someone in a game. What would you rather have them do — go *meshuggeh* and scream at you, or congratulate you for playing so well? Of course you would rather have them congratulate you. So you should do the same thing if you are the one who was defeated.

GETTING NEKAMAH

If you've been a victim of bullying, you have been suffering day after day, maybe for years, because of the cruelty of other children. The more pain you have felt, the more you have wanted *nekamah*. You have probably spent a lot of time imagining ways to get back at those who have caused you misery. You may have dreamed of torturing them or making them look like the biggest fools in history. You want to make them regret they ever even thought of picking on you. You would like them to be so afraid that they will never, ever disrespect you again.

Sometimes victims do actually carry out their desire for revenge. Sadly, they often do things that are much, much worse than whatever their bullies did to them. That is because they try to get back in one instant for all the suffering they have been enduring for months or years. If you were to succeed in getting the kind of revenge you sometimes imagine in your mind, you would probably end up in very serious trouble and may also feel terrible for what you did.

So what should you do with your desire for revenge? First, you need to understand the situation correctly:

1. You have to accept the fact that, unless you do something that might actually turn you into a criminal, you will not be able to make your bullies pay for all the pain they have caused you.

2. You want to be a winner, but every moment you spend thinking about revenge you're being a loser. Instead of enjoying yourself, you are wasting your life on angry thoughts about your bullies. This means they are defeating you. They are continuing to control your mind without even lifting a finger, and you are doing their work for them!

3. Remember that your bullies are not completely to blame for what they did to you. As you learned earlier, by becoming angry with your bullies and trying to stop them, you've actually been encouraging them to continue, just like the boy throwing breadcrumbs to the pigeons. Is it really fair to make them suffer terribly when you've unwittingly been rewarding them for being mean to you? It's like throwing bread crumbs to pigeons and then shooting them for the crime of eating them. Furthermore, if you have been telling on them to your *rebbeim*, *menahalim* or parents, you shouldn't be surprised that they want to hurt you. From their point of view, they have been *your* victims.

Now that you understand this, these are the things you should do:

1. Realize that when you seek revenge, you try to treat people as badly or even worse than they treated you. Then they will want to get back at you even more, so the war will intensify. Instead, remember Hillel's Dictum, "Don't do to others what you hate them doing to you." If you don't like what people did to you, then don't do it to them! When you treat them like friends instead of enemies, they will become friendlier, and you won't have any need to get revenge.

2. The best way to get revenge is to turn your tormenters from winners into losers. By following the advice in this book, your bullies will feel foolish whenever they try to bother you. They will be surprised and disappointed to find they can no longer defeat you. While this may not be as gratifying as seeing them driven away in an ambulance, it is a much healthier outcome for both you and them.

Not only will the need for revenge disappear, you will also have the satisfaction of feeling your bullies respect you. You may even discover that children who once used to make fun of you are now trying to become your friends! Ceasing to be the victim and improving your life is the best *nekamah*. It will make your *nefesh haElokis* proud.

APOLOGIZE

Wouldn't you just love it if your bullies were to apologize to you? If they were sincere about it, would you continue to stay angry with them? You would feel tremendous relief. Your anger would fizzle away, and you'd be happy to be their friends. Even though you may feel your bullies deserve to be seriously punished for having made you suffer, you would let them get away without punishment in return for a few words of sincere regret. That is the amazing power of an apology.

Do you have bullies who are angry with you? As you learned earlier, such bullies are not true bullies. When people are angry, they feel like victims. So the bullies that are angry with you probably believe that you are the bully and they are your victims.

Whenever two people are angry at each other, each would like the other to apologize. While they are waiting, weeks, months, or years can go by. Each one is afraid that if they apologize, it means they're admitting they're wrong, and are therefore the loser.

But this is the wrong way to think. When you apologize, you don't lose anything. You come out the winner. And the other side also wins because the state of hostility ends for them, too, and you made them feel better.

Don't be afraid that if you apologize, it means you're wrong about everything you said or did. All it needs to mean is that you regret that your action hurt them. Let's say your class had a contest for learning *mishnayos* by heart, and you won. Another student is mad at you because he worked really hard and was sure he was going to win. Just because he's angry with you for winning, it doesn't mean you shouldn't have done your best. But you can say, "I'm really sorry you're upset that I won. I didn't do it to hurt you. I'm just really good at memorizing. And you did a super job, too. I wish you *hatzlachah* next year."

Don't worry that apologizing to someone will make them upset with you. Will they think, *"Oh, so you admit you hurt me! I'm so mad at you now! I'm going to get back at you for that!"?* They'll feel relieved and will probably forgive you. They may even admire you for having the courage to be the first to apologize. And once you admit that you treated them badly, it becomes easier for them to admit that they haven't been treating you so well, either.

Apologizing is wonderful not only because it makes the other person feel better; it makes us feel better, too. Having someone mad at us can make us miserable, especially when the person is important to us. It may even make it hard to enjoy life and to concentrate on other matters. When we apologize, it is like getting rid of a big burden and we feel happier and lighter.

You may wonder why you should apologize to your bullies. After all, they are the ones picking on you, not the other way around.

If they aren't angry with you, then you have nothing to apologize for. They don't think you did anything wrong to them. But if they are angry, it means they feel like they're your victims. Is it hard to believe that they feel that you're the bad guy? If so, ask yourself: *"Do I give my bullies angry looks? When I daven, do I ask Hashem to make them get hit by a train? Do I tell on them? Do I call them names or hit them back? Do I threaten to get my big brother to beat them up? Do I tell other people how mean they are?"* Even though you feel justified doing such things, they are not helpful. They are contrary to Hillel's Dictum. They make your bullies feel justified in being angry and mean towards you. Once the cycle of anger gets started, it doesn't matter who started the conflict. If you want the conflict to end, you should apologize.

Your pride may tell you that they should apologize to you first, especially if they started the conflict or have been hurting you much more than you've been hurting

them. But don't let that get in the way. If you sit around waiting for them to apologize before you apologize, you may wait forever.

So ask your bullies if they are upset with you. They will probably say, "Yes." Then ask them sincerely what you've done to them. If they tell you, then apologize. Explain that you didn't intend to hurt them and assure them you won't do it again. And say it like you mean it.

Make your apology unconditional. That means you shouldn't say, "I'll admit I was wrong if you admit you were wrong." No one wants that kind of apology. Apologize regardless of whether the person has any intention of returning an apology.

If you apologize and the person accepts it, that's great. If not, at least you'll feel good knowing you did the right thing.

THE SMART WAY TO SAY "NO"

Throughout life, people ask us to give them things or to do things for them. It is impossible to do everything people ask of us. Furthermore, if we always try to give them what they want, they stop appreciating what we're doing for them. Instead, they come to take it for granted that we have to give them whatever they want, and they get mad at us when we have to turn them down.

If people make requests of you and you say, "No," they may become angry with you. They may feel that you are mean and don't want to make them happy. They may try harder to convince you to give them what they want, or even threaten to hurt you if you don't.

Here is a simple way to say, "No," to people so that they will be less likely to get angry or to continue nagging you:

"I wish I could give it to you (or do it for you), but I can't." Then explain why.

Once you say, "I wish I could," people can't be mad at you for not wanting to make them happy.

They can't feel you're against them because your heart is on their side. As long as you're not hurting anyone, it doesn't even matter if your reason isn't the absolute truth. If you can't think of a good reason why you're unable to fulfill their request, simply say, "I wish I could, but I can't," without further explanation. People realize you don't owe them everything they want.

You should do this with your parents, too. If they ask you to do something but you can't at the moment, don't become *chutzpadik.* Just say you wish you could do it now. Calmly explain why you can't, and tell them when you will be able to. Or if it's something you can't do at all, explain why. You'll probably find that they respect your mature manner and won't bug you.

LEARN TO LAUGH AT YOURSELF

This may sound like strange advice. You may be thinking, *"Why should I laugh at myself?"* and, *"What does it have to do with bullying?"*

One of the most famous comedians of the previous century was a (non-religious) Jew named Israel Sidney Caesar, better known as "Sid" Caesar. He said, "Learn to laugh at yourself and you will find yourself laughing at things that would make other people cry."

This means that if you can laugh at yourself, it becomes very hard for people to hurt you. The same things that might make someone else so upset that they cry will make you laugh instead.

This idea will also make it harder for anyone to bully you. As you have been learning, we become victims of bullying because we get upset when people make fun of us. If we can laugh instead, we don't become victims, and both we and the person saying the mean words end up happier. The people who make fun of us would be at least as happy if they make us laugh as if they make us cry. And they will certainly respect us more.

Have you heard the saying, "Laughter is the best medicine"? Even scientific research has shown that laughing is healthy for us. It helps us heal and makes us stronger. This means that *Hashem* wants us to laugh. It's good for us.

Do you like to laugh? Do you like jokes, humor and Purim *shpiels?* Of course you do. You probably like to hear *badchanim* at *sheva brachos.* I bet you like to read Uncle Moishy or Country Yossi.

Aish.com has a section of Jewish jokes. There are many books of Jewish humor. And there are the famous stories about the "wise men of Chelm."

But humor is not a simple, pure kind of pleasure. Consider what we laugh about. Do we laugh when people look smart? Do we laugh when they are brave or wise? Do we laugh when they are generous or strong? Do we laugh when good things happen to them?

No! We laugh when they look stupid or clumsy or miserable. We laugh when bad things happen to them. You may not have been aware of this till now, but start paying attention to the jokes, Purim *shpiels* and Chelm stories that make you laugh. Try to think of a joke that doesn't put anyone down. You won't be able to do it! You will quickly realize that when you laugh, someone is being made to look bad.

That's what humor is all about. And it's a good thing! That's why laughing feels so good and helps us recover from bad moods and from illness.

Two sides to humor

There are two sides to a sense of humor. One side is being able to laugh at other people. This is the easy side. Whenever we laugh at jokes, *badchanim* and Purim *shpiels*, we are laughing at others. Few of us have any difficulty with this.

The other side of humor is the difficult side. What is the other side? Think about it: if we're going to laugh at *other* people when *they* are made to look stupid or clumsy or miserable, who are *they* going to laugh at?

The answer, of course, is *us!* There is no such thing as a life in which only other people look bad. Sometimes we look bad, too, and it can make other people laugh. But we don't always enjoy it when other people laugh at us. And that's why the other side of humor is so important: we have to be able to laugh at ourselves. It can't only be healthy when we laugh at other people. It also has to be healthy when they laugh at us.

Why it's healthy to laugh at us

But why? Why is it healthy for people to laugh at us? That sounds like such a bad thing. To understand this, it helps to contemplate some questions.

Do you know anyone who is perfect? No! Not even Moshe Rabbeinu was perfect. Only *Hashem* is perfect.

Is it good to think we're perfect? No. That would make us super *ba'alei gaiva*. Someone who thinks he's perfect is someone who thinks he's like *Hashem*. A *ba'al gaiva* thinks he doesn't have to improve himself because he's already perfect. But *Hashem* wants us to be humble. He wants us to know that we're not perfect and there's always room to improve.

No one is perfect. We see each other's imperfections better than we see our own. If I have a big nose, if I'm overweight, if I have bad posture, if I stutter, or if I have bad breath, don't you notice these things? Of course you do. Do I really need you to make believe you don't notice my imperfections? You see them better than I do. I see what's wrong with you better than you do, and you see what's wrong with me better than I do.

Is it healthy for me to demand that everyone treat me like I'm perfect? How will I be able to fix what's wrong with me if no one tells me what it is? And if I need to be treated like I'm perfect, all anyone needs to do to get me angry is to point out what's wrong with me. And they will keep on picking on me to have the fun of seeing me getting angry and looking like a fool. If you pay attention, you'll discover that the people who get made fun of all the time are the ones who get upset when they're made fun of.

And let's say that it's actually possible to be perfect. Let's say I'm a child who gets 100 on all of my tests. I am always the first to raise a hand when the *rebbeim* and *mechanchim* ask questions. I *daven* with obvious *kavonoh* and rush to do all *mitzvos*. I am the best at all sports. I am the best looking person in the whole school and always wear the coolest clothing. Do you think you would like me better? You would probably be jealous of me and maybe even hate me. You might think I'm a snob. You might stay far away from me because whenever you're near me, you're reminded that you're not as good as me.

You see, no one is going to like me better if I'm perfect.

Who is more fun to be with? 1) People who demand to be treated like they're perfect, or 2) People who know they're not perfect and can take and make a joke about themselves? The second, of course! It's no fun to be with *ba'alei gaiva* who need to be treated like they're perfect. We have to be so careful what we say to them because we're afraid they'll get upset. We prefer being with *anavim* who can take and even make jokes about themselves. They make us laugh, and because they show that they accept their imperfections, they make it easier for us to accept our own imperfections.

The truth is that people will be more comfortable around me if I'm not perfect than if I am.

So once I realize that no one is perfect, that people see what's wrong with me better than I do, and that no one hates me because I'm imperfect, then I can relax. I will have an easier time handling criticism, and instead of getting upset or angry when people make jokes about me, I will be able to laugh. So get rid of the idea that people need us to be perfect.

Have you heard the word *teasing?* It's when we insult each other, but are not trying to cause pain. We are just trying to have fun. It's like playfighting, but with words. Compliments aren't funny. Insults are.

But some of us are too sensitive about teasing. We react as though it's an attempt to hurt us. So we get angry. We treat teasers like enemies. That, of course, makes them want to insult us even more. And this time they may truly be intending to upset us!

Life becomes a lot more enjoyable when we can laugh at each other and at ourselves. Chances are, if you have a good friend, you sometimes make fun of each other and neither one of you gets upset about it.

And that's why *Hashem* programmed us to enjoy humor. It's one of His ways of making us humble. He wants us to know that we're not perfect, that we shouldn't be *ba'alei gaiva,* that we shouldn't be overly sensitive, and that we all have things about us that can be improved. We make jokes about each other to help us realize we're not perfect and where we can use improvement.

One of the most important psychologists in history was an Austrian Jew named Sigmund Freud. He was an *apikoirus,* and not all psychologists agree with many of his ideas, but he still had many insights about life that we can learn from. One thing he said is, "The first person who hurled an insult instead of a stone was the founder of civilization." This means that if we live by our *nefesh habehamis* and we want someone to stop doing the wrong thing, we would hit the person physically. A more *mentschliche* way to get him to behave better is to insult him.

Here's a simple example. Let's say you are overweight and I'm your brother. You pull out a half-gallon of ice cream from the freezer and start eating it right out of the container. What would you rather have me do to you? 1) Hit you over the head with a heavy frying pan, or 2) Say to you, "You look like a hippopotamus! I'm going to donate you to a zoo!"

Or let's say it's Shabbos and I see you using your cell phone. What would you rather have me do? 1) Hit you over the head with a baseball bat, or 2) Say, *"Sheigetz!* What do you think you're doing?"

The second choices, of course! There may be nicer ways of helping you than insulting you, but you'd still rather be insulted than get your skull smashed. And sometimes an insult really is the best way for someone to knock sense into our heads about what we're doing wrong, especially when there's no time for long explanations.

You may have a hard time believing that *Hashem* programmed human beings to have a sense of humor. But think about it and you'll realize that humor is a basic human trait that we're born with.

When you were little, did your parents or teachers have to explain to you what's funny and when to laugh? No. We knew all by ourselves. When we were babies, we would laugh when people made ridiculous faces or strange, nonsense sounds. When we got older we started understanding jokes and laughing at them. People all over the world have a sense of humor, and they all laugh at people looking bad. No society in the world finds it funny when people look good. We're all like this because *Hashem* programmed us that way.

But now there's a really important question. What about the *issur* against embarrassing people? It is a great sin, one that Rashi said is equivalent to murder. How can it be okay to engage in humor if it involves saying things that can offend people?

That is an excellent question. Using humor in a way that doesn't hurt people's feelings is indeed a difficult thing to do. So here are some rules to make it easier to know how it can be done.

1. Jokes that make fun of everyone

There are jokes that make fun of human beings in general, or of all members of your group, so no one will feel singled out. For example, Albert Einstein, the great Jewish physicist, said, "Two things are infinite: the universe and human stupidity; and I'm not sure about the universe." Even though it makes fun of all human beings, including the listener, no one will feel offended because it doesn't single anyone out.

2. Jokes that make fun of imaginary people

Most jokes are about people who don't really exist. There is no one to be humiliated when you tell a joke like this.

There is a famous joke about a Jew who was shipwrecked on an uninhabited island and was discovered by visitors many years later. He had built two shuls. When asked why he needed two shuls, he said, "This is this one I *daven* in, and that is the one I would never step foot in." Many of the people who listen to it will recognize their own weakness. Even though we are supposed to love all our fellow Jews, so many of us have a shul we would never go to because we don't like the people who go there, its rabbi, or its *hashkofoh*.

3. Making fun of yourself

It is usually safe to make fun of yourself because no one can claim you hurt their feelings. If you have a story about a terrible mistake you made, an experience that made you miserable, or how everything you were doing went wrong, people will love to hear it, as long as you're smiling or laughing when you tell it.

Don't worry that they will lose respect for you if you make fun of yourself. Just the opposite is true. They will respect you for having the courage to make fun of yourself, so you will be a positive example for them. You will be demonstrating humility while making people feel good. When you are able to laugh at yourself, it will be easier for them to laugh at themselves, too. They may come to realize that it is also okay for them to reveal their faults, weaknesses and miserable experiences to other people. Before you know it, you'll be able to laugh at each other.

4. Making fun of other people

This is the most dangerous kind of humor because you can actually offend people, so you have to be really careful doing it. Here are some guidelines to help you.

You should only make fun of someone if you know they can take it as a joke. If you think they are too sensitive and can't handle it, don't say it. (And maybe you should get them a copy of this book.)

Never make fun of people when you are angry with them. Then it becomes a hostile attack, and they will feel offended and get angry back at you.

Only make fun of people who you actually like, and everyone knows you like them. Then they will know that you are not trying to hurt them.

Never make a joke that reveals secrets about people. That is mean and they won't find it funny. But if they know they have an imperfection and that everyone else knows it, it is safer. Let's say my friend Yossi has freckles and skin that burns easily. One day he was in the sun too long. So I say, "I almost ate Yossi's face because I thought it was a strawberry."

Lastly, only make fun of people if you allow them to make fun of you, too. There are people who love to make fun of other people, but they get angry whenever someone makes fun of them. It is not healthy to be like that, and people don't like or respect them. If you are going to dish the jokes out to other people, you have to be able to let them make jokes about you, too, without getting upset.

How to develop a sense of humor

Here's a game that you can use to get in touch with your natural sense of humor and develop it. Get together with your friends or brothers and sisters and say, "We're going to play a game. We will take turns pretending to insult each other. The rule is that no one is allowed to become angry or upset. Anyone getting angry or upset earns a point, and the person with the most points loses the game." Also, let them know that no one has to play if they don't want to. They can just watch. If adults are nearby, make sure to let them know it's a game and that no one is being hurt.

You will probably find that everyone's having great fun. No one is getting upset and you're all laughing your heads off! You will be making real, honest-to-goodness humor and discovering that you can actually enjoy being made fun of. You will become emotionally stronger and it will be harder for anyone afterwards to bully you because they won't be able to upset you.

Section Three Quiz

1. People can be happy:
    a. Only when they win all the time.
    b. Only when they lose all the time.
    c. Even when they lose.
    d. Only when they are better than everyone else.

2. Holding on to grudges is like:
    a. Eating ice cream and hoping your friend will enjoy the taste.
    b. Swallowing poison and hoping the person you're angry with will get sick.
    c. Playing basketball and hoping the other team wins.
    d. Giving money to charity and hoping poor people benefit.

3. If you lose a game, the following is the best way to treat the winners:
    a. Congratulate them for playing so well.
    b. Stick out your tongue at them.
    c. Refuse to play with them again.
    d. Agree to play with them again only if they promise to let you win next time.

4. If you actually succeeded in carrying out revenge plans against people who tormented you, you are likely to:
    a. Win everyone's admiration.
    b. Make them feel like fools.
    c. Get in trouble and feel terrible for what you did.
    d. Scare them so much they will never want to bother you ever again.

5. If you apologize to people for hurting them, they are most likely to:
    a. Think you are a *nebbish* and a loser.
    b. Become angrier with you for admitting that you hurt them.
    c. Want to hurt you.
    d. Admire your courage and forgive you.

6. Apologizing to someone who is angry with you will probably:
    a. Make both you and the other person feel better.
    b. Make both you and the other person feel worse.
    c. Make it harder for both of you to concentrate on learning.
    d. Make you feel like you have placed a heavy burden on your shoulders.

7. Apologizing to others involves:
    a. Admitting you were wrong about everything.
    b. Pretending you are sorry for what you did.
    c. Admitting you were wrong only if they admit they were wrong.
    d. Regretting having hurt them.

8. When people ask you for things:
    a. You should never give them what they want.
    b. You should always give them what they want.
    c. You can't always give them what they want.
    d. You should become angry with them.

9. Which is the smart way to say, "no" when someone asks you for something?
    a. Yell, "Stop asking me for things."
    b. Say impatiently, "Go ask your parents."
    c. Say sarcastically, "Do I look like a billionaire?"
    d. Say sincerely, "I wish I could give it to you, but I can't."

10. Menschen:
    a. Take themselves so seriously that they get upset whenever anyone criticizes or pokes fun at them.
    b. Can laugh at other people but not at themselves.
    c. Believe they are perfect.
    d. Are humble and can laugh at themselves.

11. It's okay to make jokes about people only when:
    a. You know it will hurt them.
    b. You are angry with them.
    c. You are sure it won't upset anyone.
    d. Bystanders are around to laugh at your joke.

12. If you make jokes about yourself:
    a. People will lose respect for you.
    b. You will get in trouble.
    c. No one will laugh.
    d. People will admire you for your courage and find it easier to make jokes about themselves, too.

SECTION FOUR:
SPECIFIC SITUATIONS

HOW TO HANDLE INSULTS

The single most common way that children pick on each other is by name-calling. Even most physical fights begin with insults. People call you or your mother bad names, you get mad and tell them to stop, they challenge you to make them, and before you know it fists are flying.

Until now, you've been thinking, *"Oh, no. They're making fun of me. I have to make them stop."* That's the wrong way to think. As long as you think you have to make them stop, they will continue doing it. The real reason they've been insulting you is *because* you have wanted them to stop.

The solution is very simple. It's called *Freedom of Speech!* The United States Constitution, in the First Amendment of the Bill of Rights, gives people freedom of speech. So does every democratic country. It's like the Constitutional version of the slogan, *"Sticks and stones can break my bones but words will never harm me."* Freedom of speech means that people have the right to say whatever they want, as long as their words don't directly cause harm to people's bodies, property, or freedom to live their lives as they wish.

An example of forbidden use of words is yelling "Fire!" in a crowded theater, because that will cause people to stampede and trample each other. Another is making up lies about people so that they lose their jobs. These are real crimes and whoever commits them should be punished.

If you believe that people *don't* have the right to insult you, you are denying them freedom of speech. Get rid of this belief. It's a trap. If you believe, *"They have no right to insult me!"* all kids need to do is insult you and then you become angry. And when you get angry, they'll want to insult you even more.

How would you like it if people got angry and tried to get you punished every time you said something *they* didn't like? You'd hate it. So if you want the right to say whatever *you* want without being punished, then you have to give *everyone else* the same right. You should feel fortunate to live in a country where we have the right to say what we want without being punished.

From now on you're going to tell yourself, *"If people want to make fun of me, it's perfectly okay. They can do it all day long and it doesn't bother me in the least."* If people make fun of you and you don't care, who's going to look foolish, you or they? *They* will. And who will feel foolish? *They* will. Do you mind if they look and feel foolish when they call you names? Of course not! You'll be happy. So from now on, when kids insult you, you are going to be happy. You will be the winner, they will feel foolish, and you will effortlessly stop them from insulting you.

If you have been doing the Verbal Bullying Experiment, you should already know what it is like. If you haven't been doing it, now is a great time to start.

You may even discover that when you stop getting upset by insults, they may sometimes make you laugh, especially if they're clever. As the chapter on humor explained, insults make people laugh, not compliments.

What about the issur on *lashon hora?* We aren't allowed to say bad things to or about people. So how can we give people freedom of speech? The truth is that it is wrong to speak *lashon hora.* Saying things that can make people look bad and hurt their feelings is a serious *aveira.* This means that if you want to be a good Jew, you shouldn't do it to other people. You should watch your own tongue. But that doesn't mean that you must get other people punished when they say mean things to you. If their words aren't true crimes that hurt your body or possessions, or get you kicked out of school, it is best to handle the words on your own, the way we are teaching you in this book. You can let them know sincerely how they hurt you, but don't try to get them punished.

Now we'll give you advice on responding to insults.

First, avoid insulting back. When people insult you, it is natural to want to insult them back. It can be very satisfying to give them a taste of their own medicine by responding with a craftier insult that will make them look and feel like fools. Then they won't want to risk insulting you again.

If you can do that well, fine. But you should do it without sounding angry. If you can make it seem like the person made a joke about you and you are making a joke back, that's even better.

However, there are a few reasons that this isn't a good tactic. 1) You may not be the kind of person who can come up with insults quickly and say them confidently. If you could do that, then you probably wouldn't have become a victim of bullying in the first place.

2) Your insulter may get angry in return and look for other opportunities to get back at you, maybe in worse ways. 3) Perhaps most important, it is contrary to *ve'ahavta le-re'acha kamocha*. As Hillel taught, we shouldn't do to others what we hate them doing to us. So if we don't like them insulting us, we shouldn't insult them.

There are lots of ways you can successfully respond to insults in real life situations, but they should all follow two basic rules: 1) Don't get upset; 2) Don't try to force them to stop.

Ignoring. If you do it well, ignoring can be the quickest and most effective way to stop people from insulting you. Decide that you will only respond to people when they treat you with respect. So if they insult you, act like you didn't even hear them. If you do this all the time, they will feel like fools when they insult you, and before long they won't even try.

However, you should only ignore kids if you know that they are insulting you specifically for the fun of upsetting you. Otherwise, ignoring them can be seen as rude. If kids insult you because they're angry with you or because they're trying to get you to stop doing something they think is wrong, it is not nice to ignore them. They may become even angrier and do something worse, like hitting you, to get your attention. Of course, they were the first ones to be rude, but it doesn't change the fact that you are also being rude. You want to avoid traps. Your goal is to make people like and respect you, and rudeness in return won't work.

Also, ignoring kids' insults will only work if you do so at all times. If you sometimes get upset, they will continue insulting you until you get upset.

If another *talmid* insults you during a *shiur*, you should certainly ignore them. You are there to learn, and you can get in trouble if you're caught talking. Don't worry that fellow *talmidim* will consider you rude if you don't answer them. They know perfectly well that they aren't supposed to be conducting conversations in class. They are the ones doing the wrong thing, not you. Even better, you can put your finger to your lips and quietly make a *shhhh* sound, indicating they should be quiet because they are not supposed to be talking in class.

If the insults occur outside of class, you need to decide if ignoring is the right way to go. If children are calling you names from a distance, or if they are saying things about you to each other, it's fine to ignore them. Simply mind your own business. Realize that their attention is on you, so they are making you important and powerful. You'll be the winner – as long as you're happy.

However, if they are insulting you to your face, don't walk away just so that you won't have to hear them. This will give them the impression that their behavior is bothering you, so they might follow you around, or insult you the next time they see you. Instead, actively treat them like friends. Only walk away if you need to be somewhere else.

Treating insults as friendly advice. Be grateful to people for what they say and make it clear they can do it all they want. The following responses can be used with just about any insult:

- I appreciate your opinion.
- It's so nice of you to care about me.
- Others have told me that before. Do you think there's anything I can do about it?
- I've had that problem for a long time.
- Please tell me more about it.
- Not everyone has the courage to talk to me so honestly.

Responding with a compliment. Perhaps the easiest and most effective way to respond to insults is with the opposite compliment. You will see that you catch them completely off guard and they quickly stop insulting you. They may say "Thank you!" or even compliment you in return. But you need to say the compliment sincerely. If you do it sarcastically, you are really insulting them back, so they won't like you and will continue being mean.

Here are some examples.

Teaser: You are so ugly.
You: You are one of the best looking people I know.

Teaser: You're stupid.
You: You're one of the smartest students in the class.

Teaser: Your family is poor.
You: You're so lucky your family is rich! I wish mine were, too!

Teaser: You stink.
You: You smell like a flower.

Teaser: Your mom is a terrible cook.
You: I've heard that your mother is the best cook in the neighborhood.

What you are doing with this approach is telling yourself that if kids are calling you stupid, they want you to know that they are smart. If they call you ugly, they want you to know that they're good looking. So just tell them what they want to hear and they will like you for it. They may also feel bad for having been mean when you were so nice.

Don't worry that if you answer with a compliment, they will think that you believe you are ugly or stupid, etc. All you are doing is saying something positive about them. It doesn't mean you agree that what they're saying about you is true. If other kids are listening, don't be scared that they will think badly of you. They will admire you for being so nice and mature. If anyone looks bad, it will be the one who insulted you.

Making fun of yourself. It's natural to want to insult people back. Instead, do the unexpected. Make fun of yourself instead. This is safe because no one will be angry with you. The tactic is to you insult yourself even more than they insulted you. The insulters will be thrown off guard. There's a good chance you'll get a genuine laugh out of them, so they will like you and think you're cool.

By making a joke about yourself, you are making it clear that your insulters don't have power over you. They can't upset or scare you. You aren't defensive, angry or looking for revenge. It is practically impossible for someone to feel like your enemy after you answer with jokes about yourself. But to do it successfully, you need to say it in a tone that makes it clear you're joking.

Here are some samples:

Teaser: You are so fat.
You: If you think *I'm* fat, you should see my *mother!*

Teaser: You look gross.
You: I know. Whenever I look in the mirror, the *reflection* throws up.

Teaser: You are such a geek.
You: I hope so! I've been training since birth.

Teaser: You are a real idiot.
You: My family came from Chelm.

Teaser: Your mom is a fat cow.
You: That's why we have an extra wide door to her barn!

Don't worry that people will look down at you for making jokes about yourself or your family. No one will think you mean it seriously. And don't worry that your parents will be upset with you if you make a joke at their expense. They will be happy that you can use such jokes to stop being bullied. Of course, though, the most important thing is to show respect to your parents. If you think they wouldn't like you to make such jokes about them, then don't do it.

Simple responses. So far, we've been showing you clever ways to respond to insults. You may not be good at thinking up such responses on the spur of the moment. But you don't have to. There are also simple responses you can use for any insults. Decide on one you like best and remember to use it whenever kids insult you. Before long, they will get bored and stop. Here are a few examples:

- So? (Bill Cosby teaches this response in his book for little children, *The Meanest Thing to Say.*)
- Do you believe it? (If they answer, "Yes," say, "You can believe it if you wish.")
- Your point is?
- Thanks.
- Thanks for your opinion.
- Can you repeat that, please, but louder? (Say the same thing each time they repeat the insult.)

WHAT IF THE INSULTING IS MEAN-SPIRITED?

You may be thinking that it is smart not to get upset only if kids are merely kidding around with you. But what if they're mean-spirited, meaning they really do intend to hurt your feelings? Shouldn't you get upset? Shouldn't you tell on them? Don't they deserve to be punished?

No. It doesn't matter how the kids feel when they are insulting you. They still have freedom of speech. It is your response that determines how the situation turns out. If the kids insult you in a lighthearted way but you become angry and try to make them stop, they will *become* mean-spirited. On the other hand, if they start out mean-spirited but you answer with humor, then they will laugh and *become* lighthearted.

Remember, one of the worst things you can do to people is to try to get them in trouble. You should tell the authorities only when they cause true damage to people's body or valuables or to prevent them from doing so. But you should never tell on them for calling you names. It is truly *nebbishy* to tell a teacher or principal on another *talmid* for saying a bad word to you. It doesn't matter if the insult was said in front of a bunch of children. If the insult made you look foolish, telling will make you look even more foolish. Plus, the kids will be angry with you and may want to get back at you.

INSULTING STEREOTYPES

It's easy to upset people with insulting stereotypes about their group. This is known as racism or prejudice. Today, these insults are considered especially offensive. It's easier to get people in trouble for making fun of your group than for making fun of you personally.

The belief that insulting the group you belong to is worse than insulting you personally leaves you vulnerable to attack. If kids discover they can't upset you by calling you idiot or ugly but they can get you angry by insulting your group, then that's what they will do.

If people would be blind to group differences, every group would be treated the same and there would be no stereotypes. However, it is impossible to overlook our differences. We are biologically programmed to notice them. Do you think you could look at a group of tourists from another continent and *not* notice they are different from you? Even Jews from different groups notice the differences between them. Maybe a Reform Jew won't notice any difference between a *Lubavitcher Chosid* and a *Litvisher Misnagid*, but the *Chosid* and the *Misnagid* will certainly notice those differences. So it's inevitable that people from other groups will notice how *your* group is different, and will form stereotypes.

In fact, when groups make negative stereotypes about other groups, they are often doing so from positive intentions. They are trying to protect members of their own group. It doesn't necessarily mean that what they're doing is right, but they believe it is. For instance, let's say your group has a very high standard of *kashrus*. Your *rebbeim* believe that the standards of another group are not good enough. To prevent the members of your group from *chas vechalila* eating *traif*, they let everyone know that they shouldn't buy anything with the other group's *hechsher*. The other group, of course, is probably going to be upset by the insult to their *hechsher*, but your *rebbeim* aren't doing it with the intention of hurting them. They are trying to help people be better *Yidden*. If we expect others groups to have some negative stereotypes about our groups, then it won't upset us.

If we want to be good *Yidden*, though, we must be very careful about spreading negative stereotypes about other groups. We need to be *anavim* and realize that we may not be better than other people. The stereotypes we spread can be causing real harm.

We need to be aware that everyone likes to think of their group as the best, and they tend to be sensitive about negative stereotypes about them. In fact, many fights break out over stereotypes. If someone mentions a negative stereotype about your group, your *nefesh habehamis* is likely to experience them as an enemy and respond with anger. You may even feel like hitting them. So what should you do when someone insults your group?

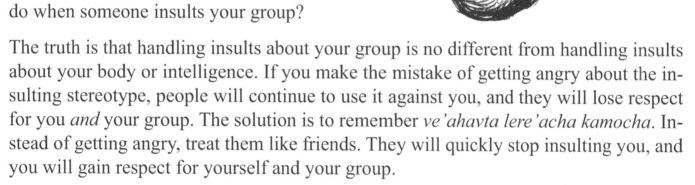

The truth is that handling insults about your group is no different from handling insults about your body or intelligence. If you make the mistake of getting angry about the insulting stereotype, people will continue to use it against you, and they will lose respect for you *and* your group. The solution is to remember *ve'ahavta lere'acha kamocha*. Instead of getting angry, treat them like friends. They will quickly stop insulting you, and you will gain respect for yourself and your group.

Let's see how it works. Let's say your ancestors actually do come from Chelm, which happens to be a real city in Poland, and everyone knows about your ancestry. Another *bochur* makes fun of you for it. First, the *nefesh habehamis way.*

Insulter: You are the dumbest kid in the school because you're from Chelm!
You: I'm not dumb! There is nothing wrong with Chelmers!
Insulter: Of course there is! Only dumb people lived in Chelm! That's why there are so many stories about their stupid acts!
You: We are not dumb! We are smart! Those stories are made up!
Insulter: No, they're not! They're true! All the dumb people from other cities were sent to live in Chelm!
You: That is not true! Stop saying that or I'll punch you in the nose!
Insulter: You see how stupid you are? You can't even think of a good defense, so you

want to hit me!

You: Shut up! I am not stupid!

Insulter: Yes, you are!

You: No, I'm not!

Insulter: Of course you are! You're from Chelm!

This way, of course, leads to endless arguing and possibly a fight. The insulter is not going to grow in respect for you or for Chelmers in general.

Now we're going to see how it could go by following the *nefesh haElokis*, treating the insulter as a friend.

Insulter: You are the dumbest kid in the school because you're from Chelm!

You: The Chelm stories are hilarious! They have made us famous!

Insulter: Famous for being stupid!

You: Some people actually believe the stories are true.

Insulter: They are, aren't they?

You: Of course not! But they're funny. Everyone loves hearing them. And whenever someone finds out that my family came from Chelm, they give me lots of attention, just like you.

Insulter: But the stories must have some truth to them, or people wouldn't have told them.

You: Maybe. There are stupid people in every city.

Insulter: Yes, there are! Even in mine.

You: Yes, and Chelm is no different.

Much better this time, isn't it!

You may think that there is little challenge to dealing with Jews from other groups who make fun of your group because you're still both Jews and care about each other. But what if an anti-Semitic *goy* is making fun of you for being a Jew? What should you do?

Of course it's harder dealing with someone who truly hates us for being Jewish. It still doesn't mean that we should respond like enemies. If we do, we will strengthen their hatred of us. Here is an example.

Anti-Semite: Hey, Jewboy! I just threw a penny down the sewer. Get down on your knees and fish it out!

Jew: Shut your mouth, you anti-Semite!

Anti-Semite: Why should I? All you Jews care about is money!

Jew: That's a dirty lie! No we don't!

Anti-Semite: Of course it's true. Everyone knows a Jew would sell his mother for a dollar.

Jew: You are really going too far! Take it back or I'm calling the authorities!

Anti-Semite: And you're crybabies too! All you do is complain and get your lawyers to sue us! And – did I forget to mention? – you have such big noses! Jews are so ugly!

Jew: Shut your mouth already! We don't have big noses!

Anti-Semite: Yes, you do! They make easy targets for our fists!

Jew: I've had enough! I'm calling the police!

This will lead to intensified hostilities and perhaps a fistfight.

The following is what might result from using our *nefesh haElokis*. The Jew will treat the anti-Semite like a friend and use humor if possible.

Anti-Semite: Hey, Jewboy! I just threw a penny down the sewer. Get down on your knees and fish it out!

Jew: Wow, it's terrible what some people think about Jews. They think we only care about money.

Anti-Semite: Because it's true, of course.

Jew: The truth is we do care about money. How about you?

Anti-Semite: I guess I do, but just a little. It's not the most important thing to me.

Jew: Health and happiness are much more important. Money only helps us get these things.

Anti-Semite: I feel the same way.

Jew: Of course! Money should never be the goal, only the means.

Anti-Semite: Anyway, you have such big noses! You're so ugly!

Jew: Do you know why Jews have big noses?

Anti-Semite: No. Why?

Jew: Because air is free!

Anti-Semite: Ha! That's a good one!

Jew: Thanks! Glad you liked it.

[Former?] Anti-Semite: Well, maybe you Jews aren't as bad I thought.

Jew: Probably not. You *goyim* aren't so bad, either!

This way is so much better and easier. All that's needed is a change in attitude.

But what if he doesn't just insult you? What if he breaks your nose? That's a crime. Inform the police. But for insults? It's a cinch to handle them on our own once we are taught how.

HOW TO HANDLE INSULTS ABOUT DISABILITIES

What if you have disabilities that are easily noticed? Perhaps you use a wheelchair, or have vision or hearing problems, or you have a learning disability or some medical condition that makes you look or act different. You notice that people often stare at you, and some children make fun of you. How should you handle it?

Your discomfort over being singled out is easy to understand. It is upsetting that life was so unfair to you. If only something could be done to forbid people from noticing your disability. Unfortunately, this is impossible.

Until now, you have probably been telling yourself, *"They have no right to look at me as though I'm some kind of freak!"* If you think this way, you will become angry whenever someone pays you too much attention. The first step is to realize that people do have the right to look at you all they want. Staring may show bad *midos,* but there are no laws against it, so there's no point in being angry when people do it.

The second step is to accept that life is not fair. For thousands of years our *chachamim* have been struggling to understand why bad things happen to *tzadikim* and good things happen to *resha'im*. Many of them tell us that the rewards and punishments will come in *olam haba,* but it's obvious that *olam hazeh* is not fair. The truth is that even if *olam hazeh* were absolutely fair, we probably wouldn't be happy. We would be terribly bored because life would be too easy. It's the challenges that make life exciting. So once you accept that life is not fair, you free yourself from unnecessary bitterness.

Hashem may have dealt you a bad hand, but don't judge by appearances. You may think others have more *mazel* than you because they don't have your problem. But you never know what problems they have that you aren't aware of. Other children can appear physically perfect and seem to be leading rich, full lives, yet feel miserable. Everyone experiences hardships in life. But if you triumph over your difficulties, you can become happier and stronger.

The most effective way to respond when someone makes fun of your disability is to let them know how lucky they are. For instance, let's say you are in a wheelchair and someone calls you a cripple. Answer, "You're so lucky you're not!" Or "I wish I could walk like you!" They'll probably regret what they said and never make fun of you again.

And don't forget that you can use humor, for it's healthier to laugh about your disabilities than to get upset. You might say something like, "If you want to look for more than five seconds, I have to charge admission." Or "My condition is contagious. You catch it by staring." And don't forget the line, "If you think *I'm* strange, you should see my *mother* (or father, sister, etc.)!" As long as people enjoy being with you, your disabilities won't be all they see.

Or let's say the insult is not about a physical ability that is easy to see, but about your intelligence. For instance, you are in special education, and kids call you "retard." If you get angry and insist, "I am not a retard!" you will look foolish, and they will continue calling you "retard." Instead, you can say, "You are so lucky you are in regular education," or, "I wish I didn't need special help in school," or, "No one would ever think that about you."

Another way to handle it is by asking, "Why do you think I'm a retard?" It can go like this:

Insulter: You're a retard!
You: Why do you think I'm a retard?
Insulter: Because you go to that special class.
You: Some people think that being in special ed means you're retarded.
Insulter: Well, isn't it true?
You: No. It's for kids with learning disabilities.
Insulter: Isn't that the same?
You: No.
Insulter: Then what is the special class for?
You: Some *talmidim* have difficulty learning some kinds of things.
Insulter: Well, isn't that the same thing as retarded?
You: No. Even very smart people can have learning disabilities. I have dyslexia. I can do everything other kids can, but letters get mixed up when I try to read. I wish I could read as easily as you can.

If you calmly respond this way, insulters will have no fun, so they'll stop after a while. They will also have more respect for you, and may stop thinking badly about students in special education.

WHEN KIDS INSULT YOUR CLOTHING

Many arguments erupt over insults about clothing. For most people, the way they dress is important because it affects the way people perceive them as well as how they feel about themselves. This is especially true for many children. They want to feel they fit in with everyone else, so they don't want their clothing to make them stick out. When fashions change, kids rush to buy the new styles and hate to be caught wearing something that is no longer "cool." Or for Jews, questions about *tznius* may be important to them, or they may belong to a Jewish group that dresses differently from other groups of Jews.

It is unhealthy to make your clothing too important. If you do, it becomes a great way for others to upset you. All they need to do is criticize or insult your clothing and you get upset. So they will continue making fun of your clothing. If this is happening to you, there are two things you can do: 1) Change your attitude about clothing. 2) Change the way you respond to remarks about your clothing.

People judge you not only by the way you dress. Your personality is far more important than your clothing. The better people get to know you, the less important your clothing becomes. You can have the coolest clothing in the world, but if you are nasty to people, they will have a poor opinion of you. On the other hand, if you wear out-of-date hand-me-downs but are funny, interesting and kind, people will think well of you.

If you enjoy dressing in the latest styles and you can afford it, that's fine. However, if you believe it is important to wear cool clothing so that people will like you, you are giving them power over you. Don't think that spending lots of money on the latest styles and hottest brand names will guarantee that people like or respect you more. The sooner you stop worrying about how you look, the sooner you become a winner.

Now, what do you do if other kids make fun of your clothing? The following is an example of how you might fall into a trap:

Cool dresser: I can't believe what nerdy sneakers you have.
You: They're not nerdy!
Cool dresser: Yes they are. Where did you buy them? Payless?
You: It's none of your business where I buy my shoes. And they're not nerdy!
Cool dresser: They sure are. Your parents are too poor to buy you cool sneakers.
You: No they're not! And don't talk about my parents!
Cool dresser: I'll talk about your parents all I want.

By defending your shoes and your parents, you automatically lose. You are treating people like enemies and acting like a sore loser, unable to accept that your clothing is not as cool as theirs.

However, you will become a winner if you treat them like friends and compliment them for having better clothing:

Cool dresser: I can't believe what nerdy sneakers you have.
You: Yeah, they are kind of nerdy. I love the way *you* dress. It's so cool.
Cool dresser: Oh, thank you. If you want, I can tell you where I shop.
You: Sure. Thanks. But I'm not sure I can afford it.

This time you turned a child who was insulting you into a friend. The amazing thing is that you didn't lose respect by acknowledging that your clothing is nerdy. The child enjoyed your compliment, and now likes you and wants to help you. Of course, if you don't really care about where other kids shop, you don't have to pretend that you do. As long as you compliment them on their clothing and don't defend yourself, they will like you and respect you. And they will stop insulting your clothing.

What should you do if the insults are not about the trendiness of your clothing but because of religious *chumras*? Let's say you are a boy who wears colorful clothing, and a very *machmir* boy who wears only black pants and white shirts puts you down. Of course, the same thing applies if you are a girl who's being insulted for the way you dress. Here's the wrong way to handle it, by getting angry and defensive.

Machmir Boy: Why do you dress like a *sheigetz?*
You: I don't dress like a *sheigetz!*
Machmir Boy: Yes, you do! Only *shgutzim* wear colorful clothing! A real Yid only wears black and white!
You: That's not true! I'm a real Yid! I always wear *tzitzis* and a *yarmulke*. And even *Yaacov Avinu* gave Yosef a colorful vest!
Machmir Boy: And that was a mistake! It made his brothers so jealous that they wanted to kill him!
You: That's not the reason they wanted to kill him!
Machmir Boy: It was part of it. Anyway, today a good Yid does not wear colorful clothing!
You: That is not true! As long as the clothing is *tzniusdik*, it can be colorful!
Machmir Boy: That makes no sense! Colorful is automatically not *tzniusdik!*
You: Yes, it is! Who says that *Hashem* only loves Jews who wear black and white?
Machmir Boy: Just look at you and me. Who will *Hashem* think is a better Yid?
You: *Hashem* looks at our hearts, not our clothing!

Machmir Boy: Then why do all the big *rabbanim* wear only black and white?
You: Leave me alone already! If you want to wear black and white, that is your business, but stop telling me how to dress!
Machmir Boy: I'm trying to help you! I want you to be a better Yid!
You: I *am* a good Yid!

This approach is obviously not going to make anything better. Whenever the boy sees you, he'll call you a *sheigetz* again.

Now, let's see what might happen if you treat him like a friend.

Machmir Boy: Why do you dress like a *sheigetz?*
You: You think I dress like a *sheigetz?*
Machmir Boy: It's obvious! You're not wearing black and white!
You: No one would mistake you for a *sheigetz.*
Machmir Boy: That's right! I dress like a *real* Yid.
You: Yes, you are more *machmir* in clothing than I am.
Machmir Boy: That's right! And you should be, too.
You: In my yeshiva, the way I dress is considered normal.
Machmir Boy: Then my yeshiva is better than yours.
You: It could be. Do you like your yeshiva?
Machmir Boy: It's really hard, but I like it.
You: So is mine, but I like it, too.
Machmir Boy: How can your yeshiva be hard if they are so *meikel* on clothing?
You: I don't know. They just don't mind colorful clothing.
Machmir Boy: That's really strange to me.
You: To me it seems normal.
Machmir Boy: I don't understand it.
You: There are lots of things I don't understand, either.

This way comes out much better, and if the boy sees you again, he probably won't mention your clothing because there's no point in it. Maybe he'll even want to have a more serious discussion about the mysteries of life.

HOW TO HANDLE RUMORS

It can be quite upsetting when people spread rumors about you behind your back, or if they tell you they heard rumors about you. The following conversation between Chana and Rivka is a typical example of how it could happen:

Chana: I heard you wet the bed last night.
Rivka: No I didn't!
Chana: But that's what everyone is saying.
Rivka: Who is saying it?
Chana: Rochel. She slept over at your house and she says you did it.
Rivka: She's a liar! I didn't wet the bed!
Chana: Why would she say it if it weren't true?
Rivka: I don't know. And I don't believe she would say it. She's my friend.
Chana: She did say it, and she's telling everyone.
Rivka: I'm going to ask her, and if she says you're lying, you're going to pay!
Chana: Are you threatening me?
Rivka: Not really. But you better stop saying I wet the bed.
Chana: But everyone is saying it. And everyone knows it's true.
Rivka: It is not true! You better not believe it!
Chana: Why shouldn't I believe it? Rochel was at your house. She wouldn't lie.
Rivka: It is not true! I haven't wet the bed since I was six!
Chana: Ha! I know you still wet the bed!

Rivka is clearly losing. She's getting nowhere in stopping Chana from talking about the rumor or believing that it's true.

What is *really* going on here? Chana is playing a game with Rivka. She gets her to fall into a trap by taking advantage of the instinct of our *nefesh habehamis* to defend us from attack. Chana brings Rivka a nasty rumor, and it horrifies her. Rivka doesn't want anyone believing it, so she argues that it's not true. She wants to win, but by defending herself she automatically loses. And the harder she tries to make the rumor stop, the more she looks and feels like she's losing, and the more Chana feels like repeating the rumor.

So what should you do if someone brings you a rumor? Don't be tricked into the trap of defending yourself. Win the game by turning the tables on the rumor-bringers. Make them defend *them*selves. How? By using the following four-word question: *"Do you believe it?"* Chana is likely to answer in one of two ways: "Yes" or "No." Here's what happens if Chana says "No":

Chana: I heard you wet the bed last night.
Rivka: Do you believe it?
Chana: Uhhh...no.
Rivka: Good.

And that's the end of that. Chana has nothing more to say about the rumor. She feels foolish for having brought it up in the first place.

Here's what happens if she answers, "Yes":

Chana: I heard you wet the bed at night.
Rivka: Do you believe it?
Chana: Yes.
Rivka: You can believe it if you like.
Chana: And I do!
Rivka: I can't stop you.

And that's usually where it ends. Chana gets stuck with nothing smart to say. If she

keeps asking if it's true, Rivka should only let her know that she has the right to believe it if she wishes. If Chana wants to believe a foolish rumor, what does that make her? Foolish, of course! And this should be perfectly fine with Rivka.

The truth is, there is nothing wrong with saying once that the rumor is not true, but you shouldn't go on about it if the rumor-bringer nags you. It goes as follows:

Chana: I heard you wet the bed at night.
Rivka: Do you believe it?
Chana: Yes.
Rivka: You can believe it if you like.
Chana: But is it true?
Rivka: No.
Chana: But Rochel says it is!
Rivka: If you want to believe her, that's your right.

You see, just don't get into an argument over whether or not it is true and you will quickly put a stop to the rumor.

You may think it is easy to deal with a rumor that isn't true. But what if it is? What should you do then?

It depends on whether people know that it's true. If the rumor-bringer has no way of knowing whether the rumor is true, there is no need to admit it's true if you don't want to. So whether the rumor is true or not, just calmly ask, "Do you believe it?" If they answer "No," you say, "Good," and if they answer, "Yes," you say, "You can believe it if you want."

If everyone knows that the rumor is true because there is proof, the situation can be more difficult. If you answer, "You can believe it if you want," they will believe it because they know it's true and will disrespect you because you don't have the courage to admit it. You are likely to feel terrible because people know something embarrassing about you and are talking about it. So what should you do to get them to stop talking about it?

Let's say that Yitzy's father is in prison because he stole money at work. The story was in the newspapers so everyone in school knows about it. Michoel then tries to pick on Yitzy by bringing him the rumor. First, Yitzy will try to deny that it's true.

Michoel: I heard that your father is in jail because he's a *gonif!*
Yitzy: That's not true!
Michoel: But my father says it was in the newspapers.
Yitzy: The newspapers lied!
Michoel: Of course that's what you would say. But newspapers don't lie.
Yitzy: Yes they do!
Michoel: I know that your father is in jail. Stop denying it. Everyone knows it's true.
Yitzy: He's not in jail! It's not true! My father would never steal!
Michoel: But he did. He went to court and the newspapers wrote about it.
Yitzy: Shut up! My father is not a *gonif!*
Michoel: If he's not in jail, how come we never see him in shul anymore?
Yitzy: He likes to *daven* at home.
Michoel: Oh, that's nonsense! I know he's in jail!

This way, Yitzy is not going to get Michoel to stop saying that his father is in prison, and it won't get him to have compassion for him or his father.

Now, he'll do it again, treating Michoel like a friend.

Michoel: I heard that your father is in jail because he's a *gonif!*
Yitzy: Yes, it's terrible.
Michoel: What happened?
Yitzy: My father explained to me that he did a terrible thing at work. He needed money to pay for my sister's *chassunah*, so he took some, thinking he'd be able to pay it back some day, and then he was caught. My father says it never pays to be dishonest with money.
Michoel: Your father is right!

Yitzy: Yes, he is. He did a terrible *aveirah*, and now the whole family is suffering.
Michoel: I feel really sorry for you.
Yitzy: Thanks. And remember never to do what my father did.

This way comes out much better. Instead of continuing to torment Yitzy with the rumor, Michoel is expressing sympathy.

So you see, if the rumor is true and everyone can easily know about it, it is foolish to try to deny it. Admit it maturely, and people will respect you more and will stop saying the rumor.

It is also important to realize that you don't actually need to answer everyone that brings you a true rumor. People are curious and often want to know things that aren't their business. If a good friend brings you the rumor about your father being in jail, then it is fine to talk to them about it. But maybe you don't want to discuss the matter with someone you hardly know. You can come out ahead by asking why they need to know. It goes as follows:

Michoel: I heard that your father is in jail because he's a *gonif*!
Yitzy: You did?
Michoel: Yes! Is it true?
Yitzy: Why do you need to know?
Michoel: I'm just curious.
Yitzy: So it's not really important for you?
Michoel: I guess not.
Yitzy: Okay.

And Michoel will probably just walk away.

What should you do if other children don't bring you the rumor directly, but a friend informs you that other people are spreading it? Handle it like Rivka:

Chana: Everyone is saying you wet the bed last night.
Rivka: Really?
Chana: Yes!
Rivka: They can say it if they want to.
Chana: Aren't you going to do anything about it?
Rivka: No.
Chana: Aren't you worried people are going to believe it?
Rivka: No.
Chana: You mean you're just going to let people spread rumors about you?
Rivka: Sure, if they want to. It's their right. I can't stop them.

This way you easily come out the winner and earn people's respect.

What should you do if you overhear people saying the rumor?

Nothing! As with insults, the freedom-of-speech rule applies. If you try to stop people from saying the rumor, they will feel they are defeating you and will show you that you can't stop them. They will also think that if it bothers you so much, it must be because it's true. So don't get upset. Don't try to find out who started the rumor. Just let them say it. They will get bored with it and look for some other interesting thing to talk about.

WHEN KIDS BRAG

It can be really annoying to be with someone who loves to brag to us. They let us know how wonderful they are, or what great things they have, to make us feel like they are better than us. And no matter how often we get annoyed or tell them to stop bragging, they continue to do it. How can we get them to stop?

When someone continues bragging to us, we don't realize it, but we are probably treating them like an enemy. Here's how it goes:

Shimon: Look at these sneakers I just got! They cost $179!
Mordechai: My sneakers are just as good as yours!
Shimon: What are you talking about? These are the latest Nikes and they're made with microscopic graphene nanotube springs!
Mordechai: Would you stop bragging already! You think everything you have is the best.
Shimon: I'm not bragging. It's just true. My sneakers are the best!
Mordechai: No, they're not! You just like to spend a lot of money on the latest junk!
Shimon: They're not junk. It just bothers you that your parents are cheap and buy everything for you on clearance!
Mordechai: That is not true! My parents aren't cheap!
Shimon: Yes, they are! Otherwise they would get you sneakers like mine!
Mordechai: Stop bragging already! I don't even like your fancy sneakers! I wouldn't wear them even if I got them for free!
Shimon: Sure! You're just jealous!
Mordechai: No, I'm not!

Do you think that Mordechai is going to get Shimon to stop bragging this way? Of course not!

Now, Mordechai will treat the braggart like a friend.

Shimon: Look at these sneakers I just got! They cost $179!

Mordechai: Wow! Those are so cool!

Shimon: Yeah! These are the latest Nikes and they're made with microscopic graphene nanotube springs!

Mordechai: That's amazing! You're so lucky you have parents who can afford to buy you the latest inventions!

Shimon: Yes, I am!

Mordechai: Yes, you are!

And this is where it will probably end. Shimon will like Mordechai for appreciating that he has great stuff, but he can't enjoy gloating over Mordechai because the bragging doesn't upset him. And he will have respect for Mordechai even though his parents don't buy him the most expensive things.

Let's say that instead of having better things, braggarts say they're better than you in some way. Again, just show how happy you are for them. Someone says, "I get better marks than you on all the tests!" Instead of answering, "That's not true! Stop bragging!" just say, "You're a really great student! That's terrific!" If someone says, "I'm a much better ball player than you!" instead of arguing about it, say, "You're one of the best players in the school!" You will make them feel good, but they'll tone down their bragging to you.

PHYSICAL ATTACKS

WARNING: *The advice here applies only when dealing with people who are basically emotionally stable. There are a small percentage of people that are extremely disturbed and dangerous. Maybe they enjoy hurting people just for the fun of it, or they think everyone is evil and deserves to be hurt. If you think they may want to hurt you, you should avoid them and make sure you have people to protect you when you are near them. If they are attacking you, you must do what you can to prevent them from hurting you. If you can't escape, fight to win if you can. As soon as possible, let the adult authorities know what happened.*

Note: *Girls sometimes are physically aggressive, but much less often than boys. When girls do engage in physical attacks, it is usually because they are seriously angry with someone that they feel hurt them. In such cases, it is important to try to find out why they are angry and to work it out so they don't need to hit you again. Because this section is so important for boys, it will be written as though it is talking to boys, but of course it also applies to girls in such situations.*

Serious fights don't just happen out of nowhere. Almost every physical fight starts with anger over words. Children call you names. You tell them to shut up. They say, "Make me!" and in a flash fists start flying. However, if you follow the advice in this book, insults will no longer make you angry, so physical fights will rarely erupt.

Some adults may tell you not to let anyone get away with hitting you. They believe children should always fight back, and that the only way to stop a bully is to stand up to him and beat him up. Here's what you should know about this advice.

1. Sometimes fighting back ends the problem. Kids discover you are dangerous, so they shouldn't mess with you. However, often it doesn't work, so you can't rely on it. You may notice that in school there are certain children who get into fights over and over again with the same kids. These fights happen *because* they fight back.

2. Fighting back is dangerous. You may get seriously hurt and instead of winning, you lose big time. Your bully is going to love getting you to fight again so he can beat you up some more. But even if you win the fight, the danger might not be over. He may be on the lookout for an opportunity to attack you when you're not looking, or he may get his friends to beat you up.

3. Fighting can get you punished by your school, so even if you win the fight, you lose. And if you injure the other student, you will probably get into *really* serious trouble. If you lose the fight, you may still get punished simply for being involved, so you come out losing double.

If parents or other adults have been encouraging you to fight and you are afraid to disobey them, don't worry. Just try the advice in this book for one week and see what happens. If it works, your parents won't have to continue telling you to fight back because no one will be bothering you anymore. They want you to win and to make kids stop hitting you, so if you can do it successfully without having to hit anyone, they will not be mad at you. They will be proud.

Rather than hitting back, use everything you're learning in this book about treating people as friends. To help you do this properly, there is an important question that will come in handy in many instances: **"Are you mad at me?"** It turns a physical situation into a verbal one. This means that you will be getting the person to talk to you instead of hit you. You will see how it works later in this section.

We will now discuss three general reasons why a "normal" kid may attack you and how to make him stop, starting with the least serious.

1. Playfighting

The boy may be trying to playfight with you. Rather than looking angry, he is probably smiling. He may even be a good friend or a brother.

Children love to playfight, especially boys, and it goes on a lot in all-boys schools. Playfighting is one of the most fun things boys can do. However, many parents and schools forbid it because they think it is dangerous, that it might lead to someone getting injured. Or they may think it is bad for the development of a Jewish child and are afraid it will lead him to grow up to be a violent adult.

When kids playfight, they are not trying to hurt each other but to have fun. Having fun together turns them into better friends. Many of your fathers and *rebbeim* probably play-fought when they were kids, and they grew up to be good, non-violent people. So they shouldn't worry too much when they see you doing it.

Why do children playfight? It's because of the *nefesh habehamis*, which is programmed for life in the jungle. Animals need to be able for fight for survival, so they are programmed to start playfighting practically from the time they're born. If you have had the opportunity to watch puppies or kittens, you probably noticed that they spend a lot of time playfighting. This way, by the time they grow up, they will have the skills and strength needed to hunt and to fight off animals that are trying to eat them. Even though we live in civilization and most of us don't have to fight in order to survive, we still have a *nefesh hanebehamis* that encourages us to playfight. We do it to try to help each other become stronger and better fighters because some day we may find ourselves in a real fight and we don't want to lose. It's also why many parents send their children to learn martial arts.

However, you may not enjoy playfighting, or maybe you just aren't interested in doing it when someone else is. So what should you do if you don't want to playfight?

First, don't fight back. If you do, you are already participating in the playfighting, so the kid will continue. Just keep telling him you don't want to playfight, until he gets the message and leaves you alone.

It might happen that your brother at home or another boy in school is trying to playfight with you, and your parent, *rebbe* or *morah* gets angry with the other boy and wants to punish him. If you let him get punished, he will probably be angry with you and may want to hurt you for real. Therefore, it is important to give the adult the following message: "It's okay, we were just playing. He didn't hurt me. Please don't punish him." This way the boy won't be angry with you, and the adult will admire you for being so mature.

It is also possible that you do want to playfight, even though the adults in charge forbid it. If you insist on playfighting, don't get upset at the adult for punishing you. Just realize it is the price you are paying for the fun of playfighting.

2. Dominance

Dominance means that the person is trying to be higher than you on the social ladder. So a kid might hit you to show everyone he's tougher than you – he can push you around and you can't stop him. Though this kind of kid may look threatening and scary, he won't appear genuinely angry because he isn't. He doesn't feel you did anything wrong to him and he's not trying to get back at you for anything.

This kid is probably not trying to hurt you. He just wants to see you getting upset, scared or angry because then he wins and his *nefesh habehamis* feels powerful. He may also be hoping to win even bigger by getting you in trouble. This is how it works. He'll push or hit you when no *rebbe* or *morah* is looking. Then you become angry and hit him back while yelling, "Get your hands off me!" Now everyone nearby, including the school staff, sees you, and you end up in trouble. The kid loves it, and will hit you frequently in the hope of getting you in trouble again.

So what should you do if someone hits or pushes you but isn't hurting you? The most important thing is not to get upset or afraid. You can act as though you didn't even notice. Or you can say, "Hey, how are you doing today? Nice to see you again!" They only want *you* to get in trouble, so they probably will not risk attacking you again, or will just do it very lightly. Again, don't get upset. Don't tell on them, either, because then they'll know they succeeded in upsetting you. Plus, they'll be angry with you for telling on them, and will look to get back at you later. But if you don't get upset, not only won't they have the pleasure of defeating you, they also won't have any reason to be angry with you. Other kids will think you are tough and mature, not a crybaby. You will gain their respect.

Think about it – do you play sports? If you are like most children, especially boys, you enjoy playing games like basketball, football, soccer and baseball. Do you ever get hurt playing these games? Sure! You're knocking into each other at high speed, getting hit with balls and tripping. If you ride a bike, and especially if you ride a skateboard or skates, you probably have fallen and gotten seriously hurt on at least a couple of occasions. Maybe you go to martial arts classes, like karate or judo, or maybe gymnastics. Chances are you have gotten hurt a few times from a hit or a fall. You are far more likely to have to go to the emergency room from engaging in sports than from being hit by a kid in school. If you can handle the pain of sports, is it too hard to handle someone in school painlessly hitting or pushing you?

What if the kid continues hitting or pushing you even though you're not getting upset? Ask, "Are you mad at me?" If he isn't, he'll realize he has no good reason to keep attacking you and will stop. Or maybe he'll just come up with a foolish reason, like he doesn't like nerds. You can respond as follows:

You: Are you mad at me?
Bully: Yes.
You: Why?
Bully: Because you're a nerd
You: You're mad at me because I'm a nerd?
Bully: Yes.
You: You mean you don't want me to be a nerd?
Bully: That's right!
You: That's so nice of you!
Bully: So stop being a nerd.
You: I don't know how to stop. I've always been a nerd.
Bully: Hang around me and you'll learn how to be cool.
You: Thanks! Do you think it will work?

Bully: Probably not.
You: Yes, it's probably hard to stop being a nerd. But thanks for offering to help me!
Bully: You're welcome!

If a kid really does hurt you, should you ignore that, too? No! No one has the right to hurt you. But before you decide how to respond to the kid, determine whether you need medical help. If you need to go the nurse's office or emergency room, do that first. The student who injured you may deserve to be punished, especially if he did it on purpose. But that can wait till later. First get the medical attention you need.

Chances are, though, that you don't need stitches or a cast. If you're in pain, simply make it clear to the attacker without getting angry. In a calm but serious voice, say something like, "Hey, you don't know your own strength! That really hurt! You must be eating vitamin-fortified *chulent/chamin*. Please be careful." It is much better to talk to your attackers by yourself than to tell an adult. You will increase the chances that they'll apologize, and your pain will soon be over.

3. Anger

The most serious reason someone might hit you is because he is angry with you. That means he feels like he's your victim. He thinks you've done something wrong to him so he wants to get back at you. When people are angry and want revenge, they can be very mean and actually try to hurt you because they believe you deserve it.

The good news is that it is usually easy to get someone who is angry with you to stop hitting you. First of all, if he's hurting you, of course you need to protect yourself and move away. Then you should ask, "Are you mad at me?" or "I must have really upset you. What did I do wrong?"

Once you ask this, the kid will probably start calming down because he feels you understand him. Then he'll tell you what you did to him. Discuss it without blaming him. Let him see that you really regret having hurt him and you want to make matters better. If you have a good reason for having done the act that hurt him, explain calmly why you did it, and avoid blaming him if possible.

And the most important thing, as you learned in Section Three, is to apologize! That's usually all it takes to fix the situation. They will stop being angry and will no longer have a reason to attack you.

Here is an example of how it works:

You: Are you mad at me?
Bully: Yes!

You: Why?

Bully: Duh! You keep telling the *rebbe* on me!

You: I guess that isn't a very nice thing to do. I'm sorry.

Bully: Well, you better not do it again.

You: Okay. From now on, if you bother me, I'll talk to you.

What if they keep on hitting you even though you're telling them it hurts? Give them this warning: "I really don't want to see you getting in trouble." This lets them know you're on their side, that you're concerned about them. If they're smart, they will stop hitting you. However, if they continue, you must do your best to avoid injury. Get away from them if you can. If you can't, yell for help. If there is no help around, then hit back if it is your only choice. In self-defense, the law allows you to do whatever is necessary to prevent being harmed.

What do you do once the fight is over? Find an opportunity to talk to the kids like friends. If they won't talk to you when you approach them, you can ask your teacher or school counselor to arrange the meeting. Then sincerely ask the kids why they attack you. If it turns into an honest discussion, great! Let them know you aren't looking to get them in trouble, but that they really hurt you and you would like them not to do it again. However, if they still insist on hurting you, they deserve to be handled by the authorities.

If the kid not only caused you pain but actually injured you, you *must* let the authorities know. Injuring people should not be thought of as "bullying"; it is a serious crime. Whoever injures people should be made to pay for their crime so they learn not to do it again and so that they can compensate their victim for the harm they caused. However, still try to see them as a friend. If you are given a chance to confront your attackers, let them know your goal is not revenge but to teach them that they're really hurting you and they can't get away with crime. They need to understand that if they continue to injure people, they may eventually end up in jail, and that would be a real shame.

WHEN KIDS CHASE YOU

Are there any kids who like to chase you in the schoolyard or on your way home? They never beat you up, but you run away because you're afraid of them, or because you just find them annoying and wish they'd stop.

What's the solution? Simple! Stop running away! The truth is that without realizing it you have actually been encouraging kids to chase you by running away from them.

You can test this out with a little experiment using a brother, sister or friend. Say, "I want to try something with you. Chase me." Then run away. You will discover they keep

chasing you as long as you run away. After a while, stop running and say, "I give up."

Now ask them to chase you again. This time just stand there. You will discover that they don't go anywhere, either. It is impossible to chase you if you aren't running away.

Don't follow this advice if the people chasing you really want to hurt you. Standing there will only make it easier for them. If you believe they truly intend to harm you, you need to run away. Get help if necessary. However, unless you have given the kids a really good reason to hate you, as by telling on them and getting them in trouble, your fear of being hurt may be exaggerated. They're probably just trying to have fun by making you afraid of them.

Instead of running away from people as though they are your enemies, tell yourself that everyone is your friend. This way you won't be scared and need to run away. Kids will like and respect you more when you stop fleeing from them.

WHEN KIDS TAKE YOUR THINGS

What should you do if kids demand you give them your possessions or forcefully take them from you?

There are various reasons that kids want to take your things, and it helps to know why they're doing it.

Are there kids who constantly take something from you, even though they end up handing it back or putting it down somewhere so you can pick it up afterwards? If so, all they are doing is playing a game with you. They want to see you getting upset, chasing them and trying to take the object back. You're trying to win by getting the object back, but you automatically lose because it is not the object that they want. They want your annoyance!

The best thing to do is wait patiently. The calmer you are, the quicker they'll return it or put it down. If you do this all the time, after a while they will stop taking things from you.

If you're dealing with a kid who's been taking your things for a very long time, he probably won't return your possession quickly the very first time you stop falling for his trap. He's still expecting you to get upset and fight to get the object back, so he'll hold on to it for a while. Eventually he'll realize you truly aren't getting annoyed any longer, and he'll give it back. Or maybe he'll throw it on the ground and walk away from it. After a couple of additional failed attempts to annoy you, he'll stop trying.

However, if kids don't return your belongings even though you are remaining calm, they should not get away with it. This is stealing, a real crime, a violation of one of the *asseres hadibros*. But don't get angry or hurry to tell on them. Let's say kids took your hat and are not giving it back. Calmly say something like, "I really do need my hat back." If they don't return it by the time you need it, you can say, "I would like my hat back, and I really don't want you to have to get in trouble." If they return the hat, fine. If they don't, then you *should* report it to the appropriate adult authorities. If it happened in school, tell the *rebbe*, *morah* or principal. If neighborhood kids took it, tell their parents or your own parents.

Sometimes kids ask you to give them something. If you simply say, "No," they may try forcefully to make you give it to them. From their point of view, you are letting them know you are against them and don't want to make them happy, so they may feel justified being angry and mean to you. Instead, it's better to treat them like friends. This means you don't get angry when they ask you for things. Remember "the smart way to say no." Respond with, "I wish I could, but I can't," and give a reason. Here are some examples:

Kid: Give me your lunch.
You: I wish I could, but I need it.

Kid: Hey, I'm really hungry.
You: I can tell. So am I. I really wish I had an extra lunch to give you.

Kid: Give me your money.
You: I wish I could, but I can't. I need it for school supplies.

If someone asks to borrow money from you, you can answer like this:

Kid: Lend me a dollar.
You: I wish I could, but I'm not allowed to lend money.

If someone borrowed money from you once before and never returned it, and then asks for another loan:

Kid: Lend me a dollar.
You: I wish I could, but you haven't returned the last dollar I lent you.

There is a chance the kids may threaten to beat you up if you don't give them what they want. Don't be scared, and answer like this:

Kid: Give me your money.
You: I wish I could, but I need it.
Kid: I'll beat you up after school if you don't give it to me.
You: I'm sure you could if you wanted to.
Kid: So give me your money.
You: I would love to, but I can't.

Before long, when they realize you're not going to give them what they want, they'll leave you alone. They are not likely to beat you up, especially if you talk to them respectfully. Your bullies, no matter how big they are, are rarely looking to hurt you unless they're angry with you. They just want to scare you. But what they truly want is respect. Everyone does. If you inform your bullies that you know they could beat you up, you make them feel good by respecting their strength. Then don't have to prove to you that they can do it.

The following is a terrific way to respond when a really tough kid asks you for something you could afford to give away. Let's say he asks you for your sandwich, and you aren't hungry:

Kid: Give me your sandwich!
You: It would be an *honor* to give you my sandwich!

And give it to him graciously. You will catch him off guard and may immediately turn him into a buddy. He was expecting you to act terrified and to sheepishly avoid giving it to him. Instead, you confidently and elegantly granted his request. You will have earned his respect and appreciation. Don't be surprised if he declines the gift and tells you, "I don't really want it. I was just testing you." You will have passed with flying colors. Let's say later he sees someone bothering you. He might go up to him and defend you. So you may have even bought yourself a bodyguard for the price of a sandwich!

This doesn't mean you should be a sucker. Let's say the kid thinks he can get away with asking you for your sandwich every day. Don't do it. But be respectful. You can say things like: "I went hungry yesterday so that you could eat, but I can't do it again"; "I think it may be your turn to give *me* a sandwich," or, "Do your parents know that you don't bring enough food to school?"

So be friendly and respectful, but don't let people take advantage of you.

WHEN KIDS ASK YOU TO DO BAD THINGS

Sometimes kids may ask you to do things that you shouldn't. The acts are either too dangerous or against the Torah. You may be afraid that they will call you "chicken" or they won't want to be your friends if you don't do what they say.

You shouldn't do things that are wrong or can get you hurt just because kids are applying social pressure on you. Just use "the smart way to say no." Let's say another *talmid* wants you to help them cheat.

Kid: Let me copy from you during the test.
You: I wish I could, but I can't afford to get in trouble.
> *or:*
I wish I could, but cheating is against the Torah.

Or let's say they're asking you to smoke cigarettes or drink *mashkeh* or use some other substance that is bad for you.

Kid: Hey, have a cigarette.
You: Thanks, but they're unhealthy.
Kid: What – are you chicken? Cigarettes are cool. A cigarette once in a while is not going to hurt you.
You: I wish I could, but too many people get addicted. I'd rather not try one.

Sometimes we don't like to admit we are too scared to do something. Let say kids ask you to do a jump that might get you injured. You don't want to do it, but you're afraid they won't respect you, so you find yourself in an uncomfortable situation.

Kids: I dare you to jump from this roof!
You: I can do it, but I don't feel like it now.
Kids: Oh, sure! We know you're just chicken.
You: I'm not chicken. I'm just not in the mood right now.
Kids: Ha, ha! Not in the mood! We know you're chicken!
You: No, I'm not!

If you continue like this, the kids will probably keep on challenging you and calling you chicken. So you might either end up jumping and risk getting hurt, or you won't do it, and they will have no respect for you.
So here's a better way.

Kids: I dare you to jump down from this roof!
You: I wish I could, but I'm scared of getting hurt.
Kids: Oh, so you're chicken.
You: This jump looks really scary. I don't know about you, but I don't want to end up in the emergency room.
Kids: So you admit it! You're chicken!
You: Sure! This jump is way too dangerous!

There's nothing wrong with admitting that you're too scared to do something. Even if they all jump from the roof without getting hurt, but you are afraid to, they will respect you more if you admit your fear maturely than if you try to deny it. You'll avoid getting hurt, and they probably won't stop being your friends. And if they do, you may be better off without friends who pressure you to do things that could get you hurt.

WHEN KIDS EXCLUDE YOU FROM THEIR GROUP

It can be painful to be excluded from a group, or a clique, as it is sometimes called. If it happens to you, you may find yourself feeling like unwanted garbage, not good enough for them. Exclusion is a favorite tactic of girls, but boys can do it just as well. What can you do about it?

If you get upset when kids exclude you, they have defeated you. They feel good while you feel like a loser. Then they *continue* excluding you because who wants a loser as a member of their group?

The secret to handling exclusion is not caring if kids do it to you. Then it can't have power over you.

"How can I just not care?" you may be wondering. It hurts to be rejected by a whole group.

The way to stop caring is by realizing it is the way to win and become more popular. If kids see you as a loser, they will want to exclude you. If they see you as a winner, they will want to include you. If you want to win, don't give the group power over you and don't care about being excluded.

You will discover a strange fact: The less you care about being accepted, the more the group will want you to join.

When kids exclude you, it makes you feel like they are evil. But they aren't. If you think of them as evil, you are giving them a good reason to want to exclude you. Why shouldn't they exclude someone who thinks of them so terribly?

But if they aren't evil, why are they excluding you? It's because everyone wants friends, and everyone wants to feel special. But it is only possible to be close friends with a small number of people. Exclusive cliques enable kids to have close relationships and to feel special at the same time. Adults do it, too. They form cliques at work, and they join various groups and organizations. They join the shul of their choice, which is also where they are likely to develop ongoing friendships.

You may wish that adults would force kids to include you in their groups. But apply *ve'ahavta lere'acha kamocha* and you'll realize it's not a good idea. Ask yourself, *"Would I like to be forced to be friends with kids I didn't choose?"* Of course not. In fact, you might go out of your way to be unfriendly to them. So if you don't want to be forced to be

114

someone else's friend, you shouldn't want other kids to be forced to be your friend. Imagine the *morah* instructing the class to stop excluding you and start being your friends. Do you really think anyone is going to respect you more? Will your classmates think, *"Wow, you're so cool! I wish the morah would tell kids to be my friends, too."* Not likely. Maybe a couple of nice kids will make an effort to be friendly to you. For most of the kids, though, the *morah* will have just made it more obvious that you are a *nebbish* with no friends.

Accept that it is perfectly okay for kids to leave you out, and that no one has to be your friend if they don't want to. Then you will walk around looking content rather than glum. Smiles attract people, while frowns repel. When you are no longer afraid of being excluded, it will become much easier for kids to want to befriend you.

Be ready to be friends with whoever is ready to treat you as one. You will find that as long as you are happy with yourself, there will be kids who are happy to be with you. If the really popular group won't include you, so what? The members of the "in" group aren't necessarily any happier than kids who are part of a more "nerdy" group. It's the quality of friendship that counts, not how cool the members act or dress.

Don't exclude yourself

If you find that you are alone all of the time, you need to check whether you are the one that's excluding you!

It may seem to you that no one likes you, and that's why they don't include you. This often happens to kids who are shy rather than outgoing. They think, *"No one makes an effort to talk to me. They probably don't like me, so I don't like them either. I'll just hang out by myself."*

But unless you are doing things that other kids don't like, it probably isn't true that they don't like you. In fact, they may think that *you* are the one who doesn't like *them*, and that's why you keep to yourself. They can't read your mind. They don't know why you aren't friendly to them.

So even if you are shy and are nervous about talking to people, don't keep to yourself. Make sure to hang around other kids, and if you feel you have nothing to say because you're not a big talker, then just listen. People who like to talk need people who like to listen. Even if you are shy, you will discover that there are kids who enjoy talking to you and may even come to see you as a good friend. As long as you are there for them, they might not even realize that you're shy and don't talk much!

WHEN KIDS PRESSURE YOU TO CHOOSE BETWEEN FRIENDS

It might happen that one of your friends says to you, "You can't be my friend if you are going to be so-and-so's friend!" Maybe they are angry with your other friend, and they want you to demonstrate loyalty by taking their side against the other. Or it could be they like to feel dominant by controlling people's friendships. This is a common tactic of girls who are seen as "queen bees." They feel powerful by controlling the friendships within the group.

It might go something like this:

Rochel: I want you to stop talking to Bracha.
You: Why?
Rochel: Because she's a real dork.
You: But Bracha's my friend.
Rochel: I don't care. If you want to be my friend, you have to stop talking to Bracha!

This puts you in an extremely uncomfortable position. You would like to continue being friends with both of them, not to lose one friendship for the sake of the other. What should you do? Should you leave Bracha?

No! The thing is, even if you do stop talking to Bracha, Rochel will not respect you. She'll be happy that she controlled you and got what she wanted, but she won't respect you because you're acting like her puppet. It's the master who gets the respect, not the puppet. And when she's in the mood for demonstrating that she's in control of the social group, she may tell other kids to stop being your friend. Plus, Rochel doesn't see you as good friend material because you leave your friends so easily. If you left Bracha so quickly because of Rochel, maybe Rochel will think you'll leave her, too, if someone pressures you to turn against her.

So what should you do?

First of all, you need to understand it's rude for one friend to try to turn you against your other friend. She's trying to turn you into a loser. Don't give her this power. Instead, recognize Rochel's tactic. She is making it seem like it's *your* choice to choose between her and Bracha. But if you choose, you lose. It's really *Rochel's* choice not to be your friend if you are going to stay Bracha's friend. So make it clear that it's her choice, as follows.

Rochel: I want you to stop talking to Bracha.
You: Why?

Rochel: Because she's a real dork.

You: If you don't want to talk to Bracha, you don't have to.

Rochel: And I don't want you to talk to her, either.

You: But she hasn't done anything wrong to me.

Rochel: Well, she did something wrong to me, and if you are my true friend, you won't talk to her.

You: I *am* your true friend, and I will always be your friend. I think you're terrific. But if you don't want to be Bracha's friend, that's definitely your right.

Rochel: But if I see you speak to Bracha again, you are not my friend anymore.

You: I will always be your friend. But if you don't want to be my friend because of Bracha, that's your right, and I will respect your decision.

Do you think Rochel will stop being your friend this way? Probably not. First, she sees that you are continuing to value her friendship, and that you respect her decisions. Since you are so friendly to her, she will be inclined to be friendly to you. Second, she doesn't control you this way, so she will respect you more. People want friends they can respect. And third, you are proving that you are good friend material. You are loyal. People can't turn you against your friends. She won't want to stop being friends with someone like you.

Another thing you can do is try to find out why Rochel is so upset with Bracha that she doesn't want anyone being her friend. Maybe you can give her advice on how to solve her problem with Bracha. Or maybe you can offer to talk to Bracha for her, and see if you can smooth things out between them. Then everyone will stay everyone's friend.

So if you want to be popular and be respected by everyone, project the attitude that you are everyone's friend, but if anyone doesn't want to be your friend because of someone else, it's their choice, not yours. You'll always come out on top.

WHEN KIDS TELL ON YOU

In Section Two of this book, you were taught that telling the adult authorities on other kids who bully you can cause the bullying to get worse; that kids will like and respect you much more if you talk to them directly like a friend about what they did to you; and that you should go to the authorities for help because you would like their advice, or because the situation is very serious, or because you are concerned that another student might be suffering and need help.

But what should you do if kids tell on *you*? Your *nefesh habehamis* is likely to respond by getting angry, defending yourself, and blaming the kid who tells on you. After all, just like it is mean for you to try to get other kids in trouble, it is mean for them to tell on you. So what should you do?

Following your *nefesh habehamis* is likely to make things worse for you. Let's say Gershon calls you an idiot, then you call him an idiot back. Gershon tells the *rebbe* on you. This is what is likely to happen.

Rebbe: Why did you call Gershon an idiot!
You: He called me an idiot *first!*
Rebbe: So why didn't you come tell me?
You: Because I'm not a tattletale!
Rebbe: Telling is not tattling.
You: Yes, it is!
Rebbe: Stop talking back. Now do the right thing and ask *mechilah* from him already.
You: He should ask *mechilah* first!

This will only get you in an argument with the *rebbe*, and it won't end well for you. A similar thing will happen if Gershon lied about you calling him an idiot and you respond by your *nefesh habehamis*. Pay attention:

Rebbe: Why did you call Gershon an idiot!
You: I didn't call him an idiot!
Rebbe: But Gershon said you did.
You: Well, Gershon's a liar!
Rebbe: Don't call Gershon a liar.
You: But he is! I didn't call him an idiot! He's always making up lies about me and you believe him!
Rebbe: I'm tired of you calling Gershon bad names! Ask *mechilah* right now or you're going to the *menahel!*
You: But I didn't do it!
Rebbe: Stop talking back to me! Go to the *menahel*!
You: I didn't call him an idiot! You are so unfair!

The *rebbe* is not likely to believe you this way, and you will just get into trouble. If Gershon hears what's going on between the *rebbe* and you, he will be very happy, and may lie about you in the future to get you in trouble again.

Here's the *nefesh haElokis* method for handling the situation.

Rebbe: Why did you call Gershon an idiot!
You (in a calm, curious tone): He said I called him an idiot?
Rebbe: Yes!

You: I don't remember doing it. I am so sorry I upset him. I will let him know I didn't mean it.

Rebbe: Good. Make sure you are careful with how you speak to people.

You: Yes, I will!

And that's it. The *rebbe* has no need to punish you because you show concern for Gershon and are willing to apologize on your own. Gershon doesn't have the fun of getting you sent to the *menahel,* so he won't make up more stories about you. And even though you didn't really call Gershon a bad name, you lose nothing by apologizing. The *rebbe* respects you for acting responsibly and for not arguing with him. You come out the winner.

Let's say that the *rebbe* insists on punishing you. Of course it's not fair, especially if you didn't do the thing you're accused of. It's still better to take the punishment maturely, without getting angry. Life isn't always fair, but if you act maturely and responsibly, the adults will rarely want to punish you. They will be more likely to start thinking that the other kids are the troublemakers, not you.

BULLYING IN CYBERSPACE

In the last couple of decades, there has been a development that is new in the history of the world: electronic communication. This includes cell phones and the Internet. The electronic world in which these exist is called cyberspace.

Cyberspace is amazing. You can get information from all over the world on any subject, including Torah, in a matter of seconds using computers, iPads and cell phones. You can spread information just as quickly. The thing that makes cyberspace so wonderful is also what makes it so dangerous. People can spread negative information or lies to whomever they want, including to you. Using cyberspace to be mean to people is called cyberbullying. Many people, especially children, suffer terribly because they are victims of cyberbullying.

A serious problem with the Internet is that it enables us to receive information that may not be good for our *neshamah*. Many *gedolim pasken* that we should not use these devices, or if we do, we should use ones that prevent us from accessing *treife* sites.

This *sefer* cannot decide for you if and how much you should be involved in cyberspace. You should rely on your parents and *rebbeim* for guidance. But in today's world, it is hard to be totally disconnected from cyberspace. Almost everyone, including children, has a cell phone so that they can stay in contact with their parents and other important people. So while we can't tell you if you should have these electronic devices, we can advise you how to use them so that you will suffer less from cyberbullying.

The most basic rule for being free from cyberbullying is to follow Hillel's teaching: not do to others what we hate them doing to us. This means that we should not post mean things about other people. Even if we are just writing a secret about someone to a friend, we can't be sure that our friend will not pass it on to his friends. Before we know it, everyone, including the person we wrote about, knows what we wrote. Now that person is angrily spreading mean stuff about us. We can end up hurting people terribly and losing friendships without intending to.

So be very careful what you write in cyberspace. It is safest not to write bad things about anyone. If you only write nice things about people, you are more likely to have only nice things written about you. This is true in all of life, not just cyberspace.

What should you do if some anonymous person has posted something mean about you? First of all, don't respond angrily or carry out investigations to find out who did it. You will look foolish and people will enjoy posting more negative things about you to upset you and turn you into a frazzled detective. So stay calm.

If you can remove the negative posting, then do so. Social media sites are making it easier for us to get rid of nasty messages, so find the instructions on how to do it.

If you can't get rid of the negative posting, you need to show that it doesn't bother you. Let people see that your attitude is that you can't stop them from saying nasty stuff about you, and if they do, it's perfectly okay with you. This will take away much of their fun, so they are less likely to do it again, and you will look tough and gain respect. And the other person will look bad, not you.

If people ask you if what they read about you is true, handle it just like any other rumor. Ask them, "Do you believe it?" If they say "No," you say "Good." If they say "Yes," respond with "You can believe it if you wish." Then you always come out the winner.

You can also respond with humor. For example, you can say an exaggerated version of the rumor. Let's say kids write that you use drugs and someone asks you about it, you can say "My whole family takes drugs together every night, including our goldfish and parakeet." Since this will sound ridiculous to them, they won't believe the part about your using drugs, either. If you don't take the rumor seriously, neither will others.

Finally, you need to realize that there is no halacha requiring you to respond to every negative thing someone writes about you. You can simply ignore it. You can also shut your cell phone so that kids don't bother you whenever they feel like. I knew a girl

whose family took her to a restaurant for her birthday. Instead of enjoying her birthday celebration, she ruined it for everyone by spending the entire time responding to nasty text messages! So learn to shut off your phone.

WHEN SIBLINGS ARE BULLIES

If you have at least one brother or sister, there is good chance that one of them torments you just about every day. Maybe even all day long. Most adults think sibling rivalry is normal. Some even believe brothers and sisters are born wanting to destroy each other, and that it's a parent's job to make sure they don't. Truth is, siblings are born loving each other. If you observe wild animals that are biologically similar to humans, like chimpanzees, gorillas and orangutans, you will see that they tend to get along very well with their siblings. Older offspring help take care of the younger ones. Watch a brood of puppies or kittens and you will notice that they play together beautifully all day long. Your brothers and sisters will get along nicely with you, too, if you follow the instructions in this book.

If you have been fighting a lot with siblings, there is a good chance that you regularly tell on each other to your parents. If you want to be friends with them, here is the first step: Stop telling on them!

Does this sound like crazy advice? Well, it's not. You will discover that when you stop telling on your siblings, they will soon stop telling on you. They will feel foolish telling on someone who never tells on them. And they will like you better when you are no longer trying to turn your parents against them. No matter how annoying they are and how often they tell on you, say to yourself: *My siblings have the right to tell on me all they want, but I will not tell on them.* If they bother you, don't get angry. Just tell them nicely that you don't like what they are doing. Remember, the right time to tell on people is when they've done something truly terrible, or to prevent them from doing so.

What if your siblings lie or make up stories about how you hurt them? Shouldn't you tell your parents on them? As difficult as it may be, don't become angry, don't defend yourself, and resist the urge to tell on them. If your parents believe their lies and want to punish you, don't get angry with *them*, either. Don't argue or yell at them for blaming you unjustly. Let's see how it goes.

First, the wrong way:

Parent: Go to your room! You can't hit your brother!
You: I didn't hit him!
Parent: Don't argue with me! You are always hitting your brother!
You: You're so unfair! He's not even hurt!
Parent: How dare you say that! Look, he's crying!
You: He's faking! You should send *him* to *his* room!
Parent: Stop talking back to me or I'll double your punishment!
You: You're so mean! You are always taking his side!
Parent: Stop talking back to me and go to your room already!

This approach can only lead to bigger trouble. Now here is a better way to handle it.

Parent: Go to your room! You can't hit your brother!
You (in a polite, concerned voice): I hit my brother?
Parent: Yes.
You: I don't remember doing it. Is he hurt?
Parent: He's crying. He must be.
You (to brother): Are you okay? I don't remember hitting you, but I'm sorry if I hurt you.
You (to parent): Would you like me to go to my room?
Parent: I guess you don't have to go this time. But don't hit your brother again.
You: Okay. Thanks!

You see, it comes out much better if you show concern for your brother instead of getting angry at your parents. And if your parents still insist on punishing you, take the punishment like a *gibor*.

Why should you take the punishment? Because it's going to make you the real winner! First of all, your siblings will be totally amazed that you are so nice to them and so strong that you can gracefully accept punishment for something you didn't do. Maybe they'll even think that the Moshiach has come! But they will also feel guilty. They know they lied and that you didn't really deserve what they did to you.

Sometimes our parents may want to punish our siblings even if we don't tell on them. Let's say they hear your siblings trying to bother you or to make fun of you. You're not getting upset, but your parents are angry with them for treating you badly and want to punish them. If they get punished, they may be mad at you because they got in trouble over you. So they'll want to be mean to you afterwards.

The best thing to do is to let your parents know there is no problem and you can deal with your brother or sister yourself. Say to your parents, "It's okay. We're just fooling around," or, *"Don't worry, I can handle this on my own,"* or something like that.

Instead of being mad, your sibling will think what you did for them was awesome. They will be grateful to you for trying to prevent them from getting in trouble, so they are likely to want to be nice to you afterwards. Best of all, your parents will be overjoyed when they see such loyalty. There is nothing that makes parents happier than seeing their children sticking up for each other, even if it is against them.

PARENTS AS BULLIES

Do your parents boss you around? Do they yell at you, blame you and punish you if you don't act like a slave obeying their every command? Are you dreaming of the day when you can leave the house and live on your own? Well, you are not alone. Many young people feel this way.

You may believe it's impossible to get your parents to treat you differently. But it's easy. Follow these instructions, and you are likely to discover that you parents are happier with you and treat you much better. And you will be happier, too.

It may seem to you that what your parents want from you is total obedience. But what they really want from you is *respect – kavod*. Even if you do everything they tell you, they will not be happy with you if you are disrespectful. On the other hand, if you have many faults and don't always do what your parents expect of you, *they will still be happy with you and treat you well as long as you show them respect.*

You may be wondering, *"Why should I give my parents respect if they are making me miserable, yelling and screaming at me all the time?"* The reason? Show them respect and they will *stop* yelling and bossing you around. Instead, they will show you respect in return.

Another reason? They *deserve* your respect. Even though you may think they're the worst parents in the world, they love you and do more for you than anyone else. Yet who do you take for granted more than anyone in the world? Probably your parents. That's because you have discovered that no matter how *chutzpadik* you are, they continue to provide you with food, clothing, a bed, and just about everything else you need. Because it is so easy to get away with disrespecting our parents, *Hashem* commands us to respect them. It's so important that He put it in the *asseres hadibros.*

If you were to speak to your friends the way you speak to your parents, you probably wouldn't have many friends. If you yelled at your *rebbeim* and *morim* the way you yell at your parents, do you think you'd remain in class very long? You'd be spending your days in the *menahel's* office! And if you disrespected the *menahel* the way you disrespect your parents, you might get sent to a psychiatrist!

It may seem to you that your parents are trying to boss you around. But do you do more for your parents, or do they do more for you? They cook and clean and shop and do your laundry and drive you around and go to work so they can make enough money to pay for all the things you need, including an expensive Jewish education. The truth is, *you* are *their* boss. *They* are working for *you!* Because they act like our servants, it is very easy for us to disrespect them.

If they are angry with you, it is only because they feel you are treating them unfairly. They slave for you, but whenever they make a simple request of you, you give them a hard time. Can you blame them for being angry?

If your parents are making you miserable, it's because you are both in the trap of getting angry with each other. Anger, as you have learned by now, usually makes the other person continue being mean. If you want your parents to stop being mean to you, show them that you're not angry with them no matter what they do.

If you find it hard to treat your parents with respect, just think about how you treat your *mechanchim*. They make you work hours a day in school, and then you go home and do more work for them. Yet you probably don't scream, curse or insult them. If you can be respectful to your *mechanchim*, you can be respectful to your parents, who love you and serve you so much more.

How do you show respect to parents? Treat them like your boss. The amazing thing is that if you do this, they will actually boss you around less! Most often, what your parents want you to do takes practically no time, and you end up doing it anyway. For instance, they ask you to take out the garbage. It takes at most a couple of minutes. Instead of doing it after they yell at you ten times, do it the first time they ask. It takes the same couple of minutes, but you save your parents the need to yell at you again and again, and you save yourself a headache as well.

Let's say they ask you to clean your room. Instead of making their blood pressure hit the ceiling for a week till you get around to doing it, do it right away. It takes the same amount of energy as doing it later, but your parents will be so proud of you. And they deserve to have you clean it. You may call it *your* room, but did you buy or rent it? No. Your parents did. It's really *their* room, and they are nice enough to let you use it. If they want you to keep it clean in exchange for free rent, it's a real bargain. So do it. It's worth it.

Do you talk to your parents rudely? With the same amount of effort, you can speak politely and prevent a needless argument over the way you talk.

If they punish you, don't argue and don't get angry. Just take your punishment like a mature person, as though you deserve it, even though you believe you don't. You will find they reduce punishment very quickly when you accept it. You saw how nicely it works in the previous section about siblings.

Even if your parents forbid you from doing what you want, tell yourself they act this way because they love and care about you. Show that you respect them and they will give you more freedom. Let's say you want them to let you go to a Purim party late in the evening. First, the wrong way to handle it:

You: I'd like to go to the Purim party tonight with my friends.
Parent: I'm sorry, but I can't let you go.
You: Why not?!
Parent: Because I said so! It's too late for someone your age. And I know what goes on at Purim parties!
You: But all my friends are going!
Parent: That's not my business. I said you can't go and that's it!
You: You're so mean! You treat me like a baby!
Parent: I'm not mean! And stop arguing with me!

Here's a better way to handle it:

You: I'd like to go to a Purim party tonight with my friends.
Parent: I'm sorry, but I can't let you go.
You: Are you worried about me?
Parent: Yes. You're too young. I know what goes on at Purim parties.
You: I really appreciate your concern for me, but I think you can trust me to stay out of trouble.
Parent: Yes, you have been acting kind of mature lately. Let me think about it.

There's no guarantee you'll get everything you want from your parents by behaving respectfully, but you can be sure you'll get much more than by being angry and *chutzpadik*. When you yell and argue, you sound like a baby, which proves to your parents you can't be trusted. But when you treat them with respect, they see you are mature. You will be amazed how much freedom and responsibility they will be willing to give you.

MECHANCHIM AS BULLIES

Are your *rebbeim* or *mechanchim* mean to you? Do they treat you worse than they treat other kids in class? Are you the one they blame whenever there is a problem? Are they dissatisfied with your work, no matter how hard you try? Does it seem like they would love to see you fail? And are you so angry with them that you wish they'd catch a flu and be absent a few weeks, *chas vechalila*?

If you're angry with *mechanchim* because they pick on you, I'd like to tell you a secret. The reason they pick on you is *because* you are angry with them. When you are

angry, you treat them like the enemy. Don't expect them to treat you nicely in return.

Mechanchim really do care about you and want you to do well. They like to see their *talmidim* learning; then they feel they're doing a good job. They are happier to give you high marks than low ones. But *mechanchim* have a difficult job and are responsible for many children all day long. If you give them a hard time by complaining or fighting them, they will not appreciate having you in their class. If you make them miserable, they will not feel motivated to make you happy.

Mechanchim deserve respect, and if you give it to them, they will like you and do their best to teach you. Think of them as your friends in school, and that's how they will treat you. Instead of getting angry with them when they treat you unfairly, remind yourself that they care about you and feel personally fulfilled when you succeed. It's possible they simply made a mistake. So don't be angry with them. No one is perfect, not even you.

Let's say you get a test back and you feel the mark was lower than you deserved. Here is the wrong way to handle your teacher:

You (crumpling up test paper and throwing it in garbage): I hate you, *morah*!
Morah: What are you doing?
You: I'm throwing away the stinking test! You're so unfair!
Morah: What are you talking about?
You: You marked me wrong and everybody else right!
Morah: Show me where.
You: The test is in the garbage.
Morah: So get it out and show me.
You: *You* get it out of the garbage!

Morah: You threw it in the garbage, not me. If you want me to look at your test, you get it out!
You: I'm not getting that rotten test out of the garbage where it belongs!
Morah: Well, maybe it's time for you to take a stroll to the *menahel's* office and tell him your story.

You see, nothing good is likely to come from treating the *morah* like an enemy. Now let's consider how it can turn out when the *morah* is treated like a good friend:

You: *Morah*, I'd like to talk to you about my test score.
Morah: Sure.
You: I'd like you to look at a few of my answers. I'm not sure, but I think you may have made some mistakes in scoring them.
Morah: Sure, I'll be happy to take a look. If I made a mistake, I'd be glad to change your mark.
You: Thanks a lot.

It's always to your advantage to treat your *mechanchim* with respect. You will be amazed at how much more they will do for you if you stop thinking of them as people who are out to get you.

WHEN OTHER KIDS ARE BULLIED

You have reached the final chapter of this book. You now know what to do when *you* are bullied. But what should you do if you see other kids being picked on?

Helping others is not a simple matter. You may have been told by school staff to stand up for kids who are being bullied. Sometimes, though, we make things worse by getting in the middle of other people's situations. These are some of the things that can happen:

1. The bullies may become angry with you for taking the other kid's side against them. They'll be mean to you, too, and may decide it's okay to get some of their friends to help them against you, too. So you may end up with extra enemies and put yourself in unnecessary danger.

2. The bullies will probably get angrier at the victim, too, for getting you against them.

3. As you understand by now, kids who get picked on a lot are not necessarily such innocent victims. Without realizing it, by getting upset and angry they have been treating their bullies like enemies and encouraging them to continue picking on them. If you take their side against their bullies, you are convincing the victims that

they are the "good guys" and the bullies are the "bad guys," so the situation will not get better.

4. You'll get in the way of the victims learning how to handle their own problems. The best people in the world to make the bullying stop are the victims themselves, because then they develop skills that will last them forever. If you stand up for them, they will learn to expect others to come to their rescue whenever anyone bothers them.

This is how it might turn out if you take the victim's side against the bully:

You (to bully): Hey, leave that kid alone!
Bully: Who do you think you are?
You: It doesn't matter. You have no right to bully anyone!
Bully: Says who?
You: Says me!
Bully: Are you going to stop me?
You: If I have to!
Bully: Just try! I'll beat both of you up!
You: You're not allowed to threaten people. I'm going to tell the principal on you!
Bully: Oh, big baby! You are going to tell.

As you can see, this approach can get you involved in the fight. The victim may like you for helping, but the bully is going to hate you. You may get yourself beat up, too, especially if the bully is a better fighter than you.

So what *should* you do when you see someone being bullied? The general rule is to put yourself on the *bully's* side and help the victim at the same time. You don't want to take sides against the bully, especially if the bully is stronger than you.

If the bully is merely insulting the victim, there is a very effective way to help: by using humor. Join the bully in insulting the victim, and then you insult yourself, too. Here is how it works:

Bully (to Victim): You are a big fat idiot!
Victim: No I'm not!
Bully: Yes you are!
You (to Victim): You *are* a big fat idiot! And so am I!

This will probably make both the victim and the bully laugh. And the victim will realize that if you can insult yourself, he shouldn't get upset about insults, either.

If the victim is being attacked physically, the situation is more dangerous, so you have to use your judgment. If you are stronger than the bully and he is afraid of you, tell him something like, "I'm sorry, but I can't let you beat up my friend." Say it calmly but firmly, without being angry. This should be enough to stop the fight.

If the bully is not afraid of you, then you have to be especially careful. As with the insults, you may be able to help by taking the bully's side while helping the victim:

You (to Bully): Boy, he must have really hurt you!
Bully: No, that wimp can't hurt me.
You: So how come you want to beat him up?
Bully: He's just a geek. He can't even take a joke.
You: Yeah, maybe not. But you're much stronger than him. I'd hate to see him get hurt. Let me talk to him and I'll see if I can stop him from getting upset so easily.
Bully: Good. He could really use that.
You: Thanks for letting him go.
Bully: No sweat. He's lucky to have a friend like you.

It may not always turn out this well, but it is certainly better and safer than trying to act like a hero rescuing victims from *resha'im*. Of course, if the situation is very serious and you are not able to stop the fight on your own, go for help.

Once the incident is over, try to help the victims learn how to solve their problem. Explain to them that they get picked on because kids have fun when they get upset. Teach them that if they stop getting upset, their bullies will eventually leave them alone. It's even better if you do the Bullying Experiments with them.

Also, find out if the victims are complaining to the school staff about the kids who are bothering them. If so, it's necessary to explain to them that it makes the kids very angry, and they should stop telling the staff unless it's about a serious situation, or because they want advice. Instead, they should talk to their bullies directly, without anger, and the situation will almost always get better.

And, of course, you can recommend that they read this book.

Section Four Quiz

1. The most common way that kids bully others is by:
   a. Hitting.
   b. Stealing.
   c. Name-calling.
   d. Spreading rumors.

2. The Constitutional solution to becoming a victim of constant insults is:
   a. The right to vote.
   b. The right to assemble.
   c. Freedom of speech.
   d. The Declaration of Independence.

3. Freedom of speech is the Constitutional version of the slogan:
   a. A rolling stone gathers no moss.
   b. A bird in the hand is worth two in the bush.
   c. He who lives in glass houses shouldn't throw stones.
   d. Sticks and stones may break my bones but words will never harm me.

4. Freedom of speech means:
   a. People have a right to say whatever they want, as long as it doesn't directly lead to physical harm.
   b. People have a right to say whatever they want as long as it is nice.
   c. People have a right to criticize the government but not to criticize individual citizens.
   d. The President can make a speech whenever he wants.

5. Freedom of speech means:
   a. There is no such thing as *loshon hora.*
   b. You are only allowed to *say* what you want, but you can't *write* it.
   c. While you don't get punished for saying mean things to people, if you want to be a good person, you shouldn't do it.
   d. You don't have to pay anyone for the right to talk.

6. If kids call you names during class, you should:
   a. Tell the teacher right away.
   b. Completely ignore them.
   c. Write down what they said and tell the teacher after class.
   d. Have your parents write a note about it to the principal.

7. Chaya calls Rivka a fatso. Rivka says, "If you think I'm fat, you should see my mother!" Chaya is most likely to:
   a. Hit her.
   b. Think she is crazy.
   c. Call her father a fatso, too.
   d. Laugh and think she's funny.

8. If kids insult your religious group:
   a. Report them to the police.
   b. Treat it like any other insult, by not getting upset and treating them like a friend.
   c. Say an even worse insult about their religious group.
   d. Tell them what they're saying isn't true.

9. If people stare at you because of a noticeable disability or flaw, you should:
   a. Tell them they have no right to stare at you.
   b. Hide so that no one can make fun of you.
   c. Wish that *Hashem* strikes them with lightning.
   d. Smile, and let them look at you all they want.

10. To be happy, you should:
   a. Believe that life doesn't always have to be fair.
   b. Always get your way in arguments.
   c. Give everyone everything they want.
   d. Insist that life always be fair.

11. If you don't wear the latest fashions:
   a. No one will want to be your friend.
   b. Everyone will laugh at you.
   c. No one else really cares.
   d. Don't even *think* of leaving the house.

12. If people spread rumors about you, you should:
    a. Tell everyone the rumors are lies.
    b. Let them.
    c. Spread rumors about them.
    d. Believe them.

13. If someone asks you if a rumor they heard about you is true, you should:
    a. Find out who started the rumor and beat them up.
    b. Say, "If you believe it, you are not my friend anymore!"
    c. Scream.
    d. Ask them, "Do you believe it?"

14. If someone hits you to annoy you and it doesn't hurt, you should:
    a. Report the incident to an adult.
    b. Say, "You have no right to put your hands on me."
    c. Make believe you didn't notice.
    d. Tell him to apologize.

15. If someone punches you and it hurts, but you are not injured, you should:
    a. Maturely say, "That really hurt! Are you mad at me?"
    b. Get him in trouble.
    c. Hit him back even harder.
    d. Cry.

16. If you want kids to stop chasing you, you should:
    a. Run away as fast as you can.
    b. Extend your leg to trip them.
    c. Throw rocks at them.
    d. Just stand in one place.

17. Someone takes your pencil without permission. What is the best way to get your pencil back?
    a. Yell, "Hey! Give me back my pencil!"
    b. Tell the teacher that the kid is a *gonif*.
    c. Calmly ask the kid, "Do you need to borrow a pencil?"
    d. Beat the kid up after school.

18. If you want to be accepted by a group of kids, the best thing to do is:
    a. Ask the school counselor to tell them to let you join.
    b. Not care if they don't accept you.
    c. Start a group of your own to make them jealous.
    d. Tell them, "I'll do anything you say if you let me join."

19. If kids create an exclusive clique that leaves you out, it is because:
    a. They are *resha'im*.
    b. They are stupid.
    c. You are a *rasha*.
    d. They want to feel special.

20. Kids who belong to a "cool" group:
    a. Are happier than kids who belong to a "nerdy" group.
    b. Are sadder than kids who belong to a "nerdy" group.
    c. Are not necessarily happier than anyone else.
    d. Are a bunch of *schmendriks*.

21. Your friend tells you to stop being friends with Aliza. You should say:
    a. "You don't have to be friends with Aliza if you don't want to."
    b. "Don't tell me who my friends should be!"
    c. "Aliza must be a real creep!"
    d. "I promise I'll never talk to her again."

22. If kids write something mean about you over the Internet, you should:
    a. Write mean stuff about them.
    b. Ignore it and only write nice things about other people.
    c. Tell the school *menahel*.
    d. Send them a virus.

23. You hit your sister and your father grounds you for a week. You yell, "You're so unfair!" and slam the door when you go into your room. Which is probably true?
    a. Your father will say, "I'm sorry I got you mad. Forget the punishment."
    b. Your father wants to be fair, so he will ground your sister, too.
    c. Your father will feel like grounding you for two weeks because you were rude and slammed the door.
    d. Your father loves your sister more than he loves you.

24. Your brother tells Mom that you hit him. Mom tells you to go to your room for the rest of the day. What is the best way to get the punishment taken away?

    a. Punch a hole in the wall.

    b. Be polite and respectful, and go quietly to your room.

    c. Tell Dad, "Mom is so mean to me. Tell her to let me out of my room."

    d. Tell Mom, "I'm not going to do any homework until you let me out of my room!"

25. If you want your siblings to stop telling on you, you should:

    a. Stop telling on them.

    b. Tell on them twice as often as they tell on you.

    c. Tell them, "If you don't stop telling on me, I'm going to punch you in the nose!"

    d. Tell your parents that your siblings are liars.

26. If your parents want to punish your brother for bothering you, you should:

    a. Tell your parents, "Thanks. He's always bothering me."

    b. Stick your tongue out at your brother.

    c. Tell your brother politely, "That should be a lesson for you."

    d. Tell your parents, "It's alright. We were just fooling around."

27. If you want your parents to treat you well, you should:

    a. Throw tantrums when they don't give you what you want.

    b. Tell them that they are much meaner than your friends' parents.

    c. Show them respect even when they punish you.

    d. Tell them you hate them.

28. You should respect your parents because:

    a. They deserve respect for all they do for you.

    b. It is a good way to get them to buy you things.

    c. Otherwise you will get punished.

    d. You want them to like you better than they like your siblings.

29. If your parents ask you to do something, you should:

    a. Make them ask you twenty times before you do it.

    b. Tell them to ask your brother or sister to do it.

    c. Tell them to stop bossing you around.

    d. Do it as soon as possible.

30. Teachers are happiest when:

    a. They give their students failing grades.

    b. Their students do well.

    c. Their students get left back so they can teach them another year.

    d. Their students get suspended.

31. If teachers are mean to you, it is probably because:

    a. They hate you.

    b. Their teachers treated them badly when they were kids.

    c. You are disrespectful to them.

    d. They didn't have time to eat breakfast.

32. When you see a kid getting upset because someone is calling him an idiot, the best thing to do is:

    a. Tell the insulter that name-calling isn't cool.

    b. Call the insulter an idiot.

    c. Hit the insulter.

    d. Tell the victim, "You *are* an idiot. And so am I!"

Quiz Answers

Section One

1. e
2. c
3. b
4. d
5. c
6. a
7. d
8. c
9. d
10. a
11. c
12. a
13. d
14. b

Section Two

1. c
2. a
3. c
4. d
5. a
6. d
7. a
8. d
9. c
10. d
11. a
12. d
13. a
14. c
15. d
16. b
17. d
18. a
19. c
20. b
21. a
22. c
23. d
24. b
25. d
26. d

Section Three

1. c
2. b
3. a
4. c
5. d
6. a
7. d
8. c
9. d
10. d
11. c
12. d

Section Four

1. c
2. c
3. d
4. a
5. c
6. b
7. d
8. b
9. d
10. a
11. c
12. b
13. d
14. d
15. a
16. d
17. c
18. b
19. d
20. c
21. a
22. b
23. c
24. b
25. a
26. d
27. c
28. a
29. d
30. b
31. c
32. d

Products and Services

How to order additional copies of Bullies to Buddies: A Torah Guide for Turning Your Enemies into Friends

For single orders, go to Amazon.com

This book can also be used as a social skills textbook in school. Could you imagine what would happen to your school if all the children were to learn the simple wisdom it contains? Substantial discounts are available for bulk purchases. Contact Izzy Kalman directly at izzy@bullies2buddies.com for more information, or to place an order.

Materials, products and writings

Izzy Kalman has produced numerous materials and products for dealing with bullying and relationship problems throughout one's lifetime. Some are available for free, some for purchase. To discover what he has to offer, visit IzzyKalman.com or Bullies2Buddies.com.

For a treasure trove of unconventional articles dealing with bullying and related subjects, visit Izzy Kalman's Psychology Today blog, Resilience to Bullying: PsychologyToday.com/us/blog/resilience-bullying.

Trainings and Presentations for Schools and Organizations

Izzy Kalman currently resides in Israel, but comes to the US once or twice a year to work with schools and organizations. Virtual trainings are less costly and can be conducted any time of the year.

Izzy Kalman's workshops are highly entertaining, as he makes extensive use of improvisational roleplaying with audience members. He is available to conduct presentations on bullying, anger control and relationship problems for any type of organization.

For more information, and to book Izzy, visit izzykalman.com, or write to izzy@bullies2buddies.com.

Trainings for mental health professionals

Izzy Kalman has developed a uniquely quick, fun and effective system for helping clients solve their problems with bullying, anger control and relationship difficulties. He has taught his method to tens of thousands of professionals at full-day seminars throughout the US and abroad.

Mental health professionals who want to enhance their effectiveness can be trained in individual sessions with Izzy via computer conference. If they wish, they can work to attain certification as Bullies to Buddies Trainers.

Izzy has also produced a comprehensive online course for independent study, Treating Victims of Bullying, available on Udemy.com. To request discount coupons, write to izzy@bullies2buddies.com.

Individual Consultation
Victims of bullying
Are you or your child being bullied? Izzy is the master at teaching people how to stop being victimized. Despite the suffering caused by bullying, it is often a simple problem to solve with the right approach. No need for months or years of in-depth therapy.

Sibling rivalry
One of the most common yet serious problems plaguing families is hostility among children. When children fight constantly, parents usually invest great deals of time and effort in trying to keep the peace, to no avail. For most families, Izzy Kalman's approach can quickly and dramatically improve relationships among children while making parents' lives easier.

Defiant children
If you have more than one child, there is a good chance that one of them has become expert at making you miserable. There is also a good chance that the same child who behaves like a monster at home is an angel in school and at other people's houses. If this is your situation, Izzy can quickly take the mystery out of this phenomenon and teach you how to get your child to be more of an angel at home, too.

Good marriages gone bad
Many marriages start out well. Initially husband and wife feel like they are bashert and get along wonderfully. At one point they begin arguing and fighting regularly, and don't understand why their spouse treats them so badly. If they are both decent, responsible people who are liked and respected by others, and they haven't strayed, Izzy's method may be able to bring them back to their bashert status in a few sessions.

Couples can also be helped by watching his video program, From Soulmates to Cellmates: Let the Golden Rule Save Your Marriage, available for purchase on izzykalman.com.

Workplace hostilities

Many of us spend more time at work than we do with our families at home. Interpersonal problems on the job can make us miserable 24/7. Business partners sometimes get into an unnecessary state of war that tears the business apart.

Don't allow relationship difficulties at work destroy your life or business. In most cases, Izzy Kalman's approach can turn matters around.

Izzy's video program, Turning Workplace Hostility into Harmony, is available for sale on izzykalman.com.

What professionals say about Izzy Kalman's work

Every teacher and administrator should hear your presentation! – Denise Donohue, Counselor, Las Vegas, Nevada

By far the best seminar I've ever attended! I wish I would have been taught these things much earlier in my career. – Steve Weaver, Social Worker, Tampa, Florida

As a counselor in a building of over 600 fourth and fifth graders, I refer to the Bullies to Buddies program frequently because it teaches students easy to implement strategies to handle being "picked on" in a time effective, fun way. The program empowers students by teaching them how to solve problems on their own. … Izzy's "Magic responses" … have reduced the time spent reacting to interpersonal problems and putting "emotional band-aids" on kids… Since our school has adopted this program students are spending more time in their classrooms and less time in the office. – Chris Robinson, School Counselor, Fairborn Intermediate School, Fairborn, OH

I went to your seminar about 2 years ago. I have been using your techniques with mildly & moderately mentally retarded men. It has worked wonderfully. - Randal Adair, M.Ed.

Izzy's message is right on and needs to get out to all therapists, educators, and other human service personnel. This may be the best one day workshop I have attended in 40 years of being a mental health professional. Thanks, Izzy. Jim Werner, Counselor, St. Cloud, Minnesota

Loved it! Izzy was very entertaining as well as informative. This is the best continuing education seminar I've ever been to. I liked the role playing and Izzy's willingness to take on any situation thrown at him by the audience. – Angela Gilbert, Licensed Psychological Examiner, Little Rock, Arkansas

Excellent seminar! Lots of food for thought – turns the whole concept of bully-reduction program, strategies and conceptualization on its head. – Heather Eaton, Marriage and Family Therapist, Irvine, California

This is one of the best workshops I've ever attended. It is turning my views on bullying upside down. I will be totally re-vamping my program on this topic. I found the role-plays extremely useful. – Lynn Bohlmann, Social Worker/Counselor, Seattle, Washington

This is the best workshop I've been to in years! Thanks for giving me a new way to look at and explain anger. I will use it right away – both in my personal and professional life. I really loved the role-playing. It's so tangible – I can take it back to work tomorrow to use and teach to teachers, principal as well as students. – Trudy Kent, Counselor, Boise, Idaho

This is the best professional seminar I have attended. I'm leaving with great tools to use with children in the social skills group I facilitate. Additionally, these tools and perspectives are valuable to use in other areas of my life. – June Matthews, Social Worker, Orlando, Florida

The very best presentation/content of any seminar I have attended ever! – James Conaway, Educator/Psychologist, Philadelphia, Pennsylvania

Wow! My brain is full of some really good stuff right now! You have clarified why I was uncomfortable with aspects of currently used materials. I can't wait to go back and use what I've learned. Thank you, Izzy!
– Karen Sturdevant, Counselor, Madison, Wisconsin

Made in the USA
Middletown, DE
20 February 2024

49925738R00084